CONSERVATISM
IN EUROPE
1770–1945

For Barbara,
With love for the best,
John
3/9/77.

D1253544

CONSERVATISM IN EUROPE

1770–1945

TRADITIONALISM, REACTION AND COUNTER-REVOLUTION

JOHN WEISS

with 50 illustrations

THAMES AND HUDSON · LONDON

For Barbara, Elizabeth and Paul

1   Frontispiece, *The Holy Alliance*,
gouache by Heinrich Olivier, 1815. In
an imaginary medieval setting,
Alexander I of Russia, Francis I of
Austria and Frederick William III of
Prussia pledge themselves to defend the
'Christian nation' of Europe.

Picture research by Georgina Bruckner

Printed and bound in Great Britain by
Jarrold and Sons Ltd, Norwich

CONTENTS

AUTHOR'S PREFACE

Much has been written about liberalism in Europe, little about conservatism. This book is an attempt to restore the balance. It begins before the Revolution of 1789, and carries the story to 1945. Throughout, I have assumed that a conservative is a person who hopes to preserve or restore some significant part of the political structures, social arrangements, economic relationships or cultural values of the past.

Conservatives have exercised more power in Europe than is generally supposed. This book tries to show how they won the support of a wide variety of groups and classes, and how their ideas and values evolved in response to changing social circumstances. Ideas help cause social change to the extent that they are adopted by broad interest groups competing for power. Conservative values are adopted by those who feel threatened by social modernization. If some well-known and brilliant conservative thinkers have been omitted (Jacob Burckhardt is one), that is because the subtlety of their thought prevented them from having direct influence on major social movements. If conservatives of considerably less intellectual distinction have been dealt with at some length (Heinrich von Treitschke, for example), it is because they became spokesmen for powerful trends and movements which transcended their own work. Thus Treitschke was the popularizer of Bismarck's conservative policy of 'blood and iron'. The book ends with the 1939–45 war because the latter marks the end of any significant potential for success in Europe of either traditional conservatism or its extreme right-wing variant, fascism.

Since the ideology and politics of conservatism in Great Britain, Italy, Spain and Portugal were quite different from those in Germany, France and the Austrian Empire, they have been excluded. To do justice to those differences would require a manuscript far exceeding the limits required by this series.

I wish to acknowledge the excellent editorial guidance of Professor Geoffrey Barraclough. Any errors of fact or interpretation are, of course, my own.

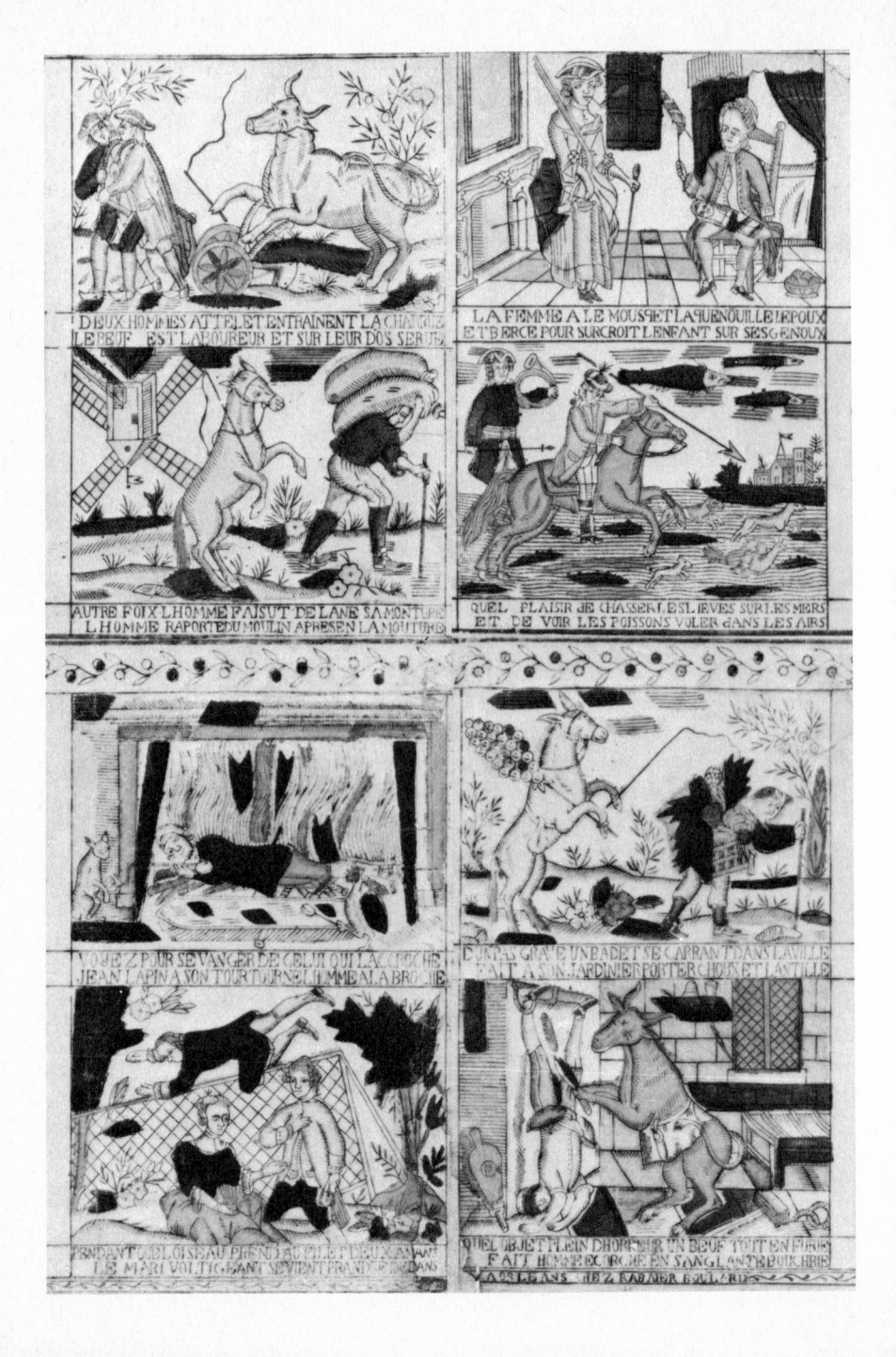

I CONSERVATISM IN EARLY MODERN EUROPE

The conservative response to modernization did not, as is often held, begin with the French Revolution; it began with the threats posed to the traditional order of Europe by princes in the seventeenth and eighteenth centuries. To centralize and increase their authority, a number of princes, with varying degrees of success, sought to reduce the powers and privileges of the nobles, urban patricians, the Church hierarchy, guild masters and other semi-feudal corporate institutions. These groups responded in defence of the old ways. State-building was the great political business of early modern Europe, and was often a matter of survival. There was not a decade of peace in these centuries; indeed, the modern state was made for war. Increasingly, successful rulers were able to wrest relatively unencumbered control of their armies, their laws, their bureaucracies and their nations' wealth from aristocrats and privileged institutions. Louis XIV expressed the prince's ideal: 'It is in my person alone that the sovereign power resides . . . It is to me alone that the legislative power appertains . . . the rights and interests of the nation . . . are necessarily united with mine and rest exclusively in my hands . . . I am the state.' Conversely, where great nobles were able to maintain their ancient liberties and thwart the prince, the state was in grave danger of the fate that befell Poland by the end of the eighteenth century—it was partitioned and annexed *in toto* by Prussia, Russia and Austria.

In self-defence, the aristocracies of Europe advanced the oldest and most enduring of conservative ideas: the state must not be allowed to expand its powers at the expense of local groups and corporate interests. In many states aristocratic families had been rewarded for service, or had purchased judicial, military, administrative and financial positions which made them independent and which could be passed on to their heirs. But princes needed civil servants whom they could appoint, dismiss or promote at will; men who could be held accountable for specific tasks and who followed political and legal standards: men, in short, who knew that the path to preferment lay in the gratitude of princes. So it was in France that the ancient nobility who had once overawed the throne were gradually reduced

2 'The folly of men or the world turned upside down.' Animals triumph over men in a reversal of the order of nature. French popular print of the mid-eighteenth century.

to fighting petty battles for pensions in the midst of the ceremonial rituals of personal service and submission to the Crown at Versailles. In the provinces aristocratic governors were replaced by direct agents of the king. Noble magistrates and judicial officials lost their influence over legislation. Military officers were subjected to royal command.

In Prussia a similar process began with the reign of the Great Elector, Frederick William, in 1640. His domains had been ravaged by the Thirty Years War (1618–48). His principal towns lay in ruins; his population was reduced by more than a third. Yet he could neither raise nor pay troops without the permission of his nobles, who wished only to protect their particular territories. The Great Elector co-opted, imprisoned or killed their leaders. Thus tamed, the Junkers of Prussia became the most efficient and loyal servants of any European prince. There was a price, however: in return the Junkers gained the right to monopolize the highest offices of state and army, and unlimited power to exploit their serfs. The ancient noble families of France gained fiscal and tax exemptions that helped push France to the verge of bankruptcy in the 1780s.

In Spain, Portugal and Sweden there were similar confrontations between prince and nobles, with noble powers usually weakened. In the Austrian Empire, however, and in spite of the efforts of the most revolutionary of enlightened despots, Joseph II, a conservative counter-revolution restored almost every local office and government institution to noble hands by the end of the eighteenth century.

Many voices were raised in defence of the embattled aristocracy and against the tyranny of princes and their intellectual allies, the *philosophes*. Some of the most influential thinkers of the Enlightenment, including Voltaire, hoped to see the debris of feudal particularism swept away so that the rational norms of enlightened princes might apply throughout Europe. Because it was the fount of liberal values, later generations have called the eighteenth century the age of Enlightenment. It is well to remember that, in quantity at least, more was published against than in favour of the principles of the *philosophes*.

Among the most influential conservative spokesmen were the famous Montesquieu and the now barely remembered Justus Möser. The Baron de Montesquieu's mighty *De l'esprit des lois* transcends mere politics, but contemporaries recognized in it a sophisticated voice for the reaction. Himself a noble who had inherited judicial

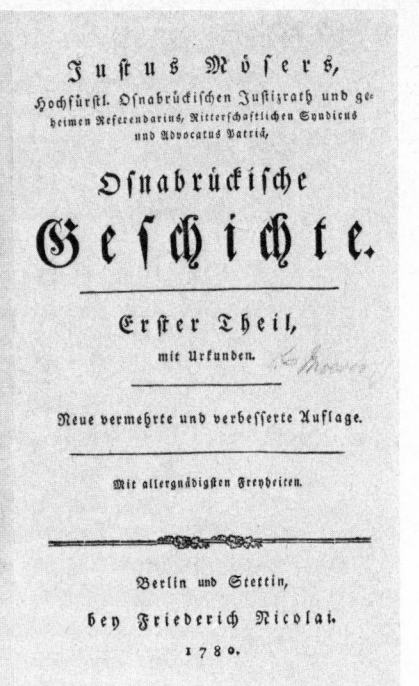

3 Title-page of Justus Möser's *History of Osnabrück*, Berlin 1780. First published in 1768, this work traced the influence of folk traditions on community customs and government.

office, Montesquieu argued that only an inherited system of office-holding could protect the citizen from arbitrary princely despotism. It was, he argued, one way of preserving the scattered centres and institutions of power which he called the *corps intermédiaire*. Montesquieu admitted the defects of choice by birth, but questioned whether frail reason could invent a better system. Failing republican institutions, open competition for office would have to be on terms set by the prince; what could this mean but the rise to power of the most abject sycophants?

Justus Möser (1720–94) had an enduring influence on nineteenth-century conservative thought. He was the first minister, appropriately enough, of the ruling oligarchy of the tiny sovereignty of Osnabrück, often called a veritable museum of the German medieval past, with its complex pattern of overlapping feudal jurisdictions among aristocrats, oligarchs and clerics. Möser treasured feudal particularism and denounced the 'reckless innovators' who trampled

4　*The Devil and the Estates.* Society represented by the stock figures of king, clergy, soldier, monk, peasant, Jew, actor and whore. Oil painting by an unknown artist, Trier, second half of the eighteenth century.

upon customs, rights, and habits which, he argued, were the product of an ancient and instinctive *Volk* wisdom pre-eminently adapted to local needs and diverse conditions. To those who argued, with Bishop Bossuet, for the divine right of kings, Möser countered that the entire social order was divine. Did not each estate in the social hierarchy possess its sacred traditional rights and duties in a delicately balanced organic whole? Men should not seek their standards for society in the abstract and consciously reasoned notions of so-called universal natural laws; instead they should observe the actual creations of God and man in time.

To increase revenues and production, many princes sought to replace complex feudal regulations and customs which hampered economic progress with their own innovations, while physiocrats called for the freeing of trade from restrictions. Princes built canals, roads and dams, reclaimed lands and attempted to end some of the fiscal privileges of nobles and corporate institutions. Joseph II even hoped to tax all, regardless of social class. Aristocratic interests were also threatened by attempts to end internal customs dues and break up entailed estates. Villagers, comfortable in their ancestral ways, were often upset and sometimes harmed when forced to introduce new techniques and the system of cash crops for distant markets. Guildsmen objected when new enterprises not subject to their regulations were founded, and when guilds were required to relax their controls over who should produce what products for which markets, and at what price and wage rates.

Möser praised the traditional and regulated stability of the village and guild. One could feel secure with a fixed sense of task and status, and one could know the future through the past. Why sacrifice communal stability and long-established relationships to the unlimited aggression of materialistic 'free' enterprise, or the power drives of avaricious princes and bureaucrats? As a citizen of Osnabrück, Möser especially feared the disappearance of the rich variety of customs and political forms of feudal particularism. He even defended serfdom, albeit reluctantly, and without the simple racism of many contemporaries who held that the nobles had subjected the serfs by right of conquest, and that it would be futile to attempt to improve the lot of those inferior by nature. Möser preferred to idealize the healthy, natural, stable and pious life of the serf.

In his general regard for feudal particularism, Möser expressed a common conservative attitude: the wish to leave undisturbed unique ways of life he would not wish to share. Montesquieu's pioneering work in sociology, with its emphasis on the necessity and rightness of variety in social sub-groups, expressed a similar conservative viewpoint. Conservatives, hoping to preserve their estates within the state, naturally tended to stress the rationale for social diversity, rather than the overriding claims of universal natural law advanced by the *philosophes*.

Montesquieu's cultural relativism reveals his conservative stance: each society must be shaped by local peculiarities of geography, climate and race. Each form of government should be imbued with a corresponding form of the human spirit. The citizens of a republic, in his famous distinction, must possess the virtue of sacrifice for the community; Oriental despotisms based their power upon their subjects' fear. To the delight of his aristocratic readers, Montesquieu insisted that a monarchy must be supported by an independent and thriving nobility, who possessed the virtues of pride, dignity and honour, and were the mainstay of public service.

Before the eighteenth century, all world-views had to accommodate themselves to theology; with the advent of Newton and Locke, science in the West became the foremost model for political theory. Using a simplified Cartesianism, the princes' defenders held that the universe was a mechanism of clashing atoms and whirling vortices which could only be set in order by the guidance of divine reason. Did not the prince, they argued, also function as the one who must give order and law to the clashing individual wills of society? Was it not in this sense that the prince ruled by divine right? Conservatives countered with the traditional Aristotelian-Christian world-view. The social order was not a mere anarchy; it was composed, as was the order of nature, of self-developing organisms endowed with unique and essential qualities which allowed the unfolding of the harmonious grand design, whose final cause was the will of God. Society was not just a mass of equal individuals locked in a war of all against all, requiring an order dictated by the prince. Each estate had its unique and innate principle: the inborn sense of honour of the noble, the embodiment of the drama of salvation which was the Church, the self-regulation of the guildsman and the dignified humility of the serf. These were the estates created by infinite wisdom in the divine plan of hierarchy and harmony. How absurd, conservatives argued, to imagine that society could be improved by the tinkering frailties of the finite human intellect.

Today we can hardly remember a time without social change and rational planning. Möser and his fellow conservatives defended what they took to be society itself – not merely a possible version of society. Although they created the basic elements of nineteenth-century conservative ideology, they did not see themselves as theorists. Soon their ideas would be put to new uses, for prince, noble, priest and guildsman were to be caught up in the dramatic upheavals of the revolutionary era.

II THE FRENCH REVOLUTION

The aristocrats themselves precipitated the Revolution by their resistance to reform. By the late 1780s France faced bankruptcy, while falling real wages, rising inflation, increasing feudal burdens and bad harvests made it impossible to squeeze more from the common people. The finance ministers of the King, Necker and Calonne, knew that it would be necessary to tax aristocratic incomes and abolish some of the exemptions of the privileged. To increase economic productivity, moreover, some guild restrictions would have to be removed and the feudal burdens of the peasantry lightened. The nobility of France were not willing even to consider such threats to their interests. To them, feudal dues and fiscal exemptions were rights which adhered to inherited status. All French bishops were nobles, and this reinforced the Church's refusal to be taxed. Indeed, in 1788 the Church gave the treasury the smallest 'voluntary donation' it had given in decades. However, the nobles did call for a meeting of the Estates-General. They assumed they could easily dominate it.

Few realized how rapidly liberal and reforming ideas had gained support during the course of the eighteenth century. Dramatic increases in colonial and domestic trade and the expansion of government activities had brought new and politically conscious men to the fore: lawyers, lesser magistrates, civil servants, men in commerce and trade, non-titled property-owners and other professional classes. Often their careers were blocked because of their non-noble origins. Many found themselves treated with contempt by the privileged. In turn, these new men found little to respect in a parasitic nobility and a Church which by the late eighteenth century was renowned for its greed and lack of piety. The elected representatives of the Third Estate came from such groups. When the aristocracy and upper clergy, following legal precedent, tried to assert their ancient right to outvote the Third Estate two to one, the Third Estate retaliated. It declared itself the National Assembly and as such the sole representative of the nation in June 1789.

The ideas of the new leaders were best expressed in the widely read pamphlet, *Qu'est-ce que le tiers état?*, written by the Abbé Sieyès. Himself elected to the Third Estate, Sieyès led the battle against nobles and clerics, guided much of the Assembly's legislation, was a member of the government throughout the 1790s – and even stage-managed Napoleon's *coup* in 1799. Simplifying the ideas of the liberal *philosophes*, Sieyès held that the Third Estate included all the truly productive classes of the nation; indeed, it *was* the nation. What were the nobles except highly paid parasites who had placed their interests and thus themselves outside the nation? True foreigners, they used high office to maintain their private privileges, labelled honest work degrading and claimed that they, a mere 200,000, represented 26 million Frenchmen. A nation, Sieyès insisted, was a society of equals based on consent; its sovereignty was inalienable and, even if it wished to, it could not yield its collective rights in perpetuity to any private group. There could be no estates, orders, aristocracies or guilds. All private powers must be surrendered to the National Assembly; it in turn must provide a constitution and a government elected to represent the public interest: a government which would treat all equally under the law. It should be understood, however, that Sieyès did not speak for the masses without property. He spoke for the bureaucratic, professional and commercial classes mentioned above, as well as for the small peasant proprietors suffering from feudal burdens. Once rid of the system of inherited privilege, Sieyès assumed, as did all early liberals, that a bourgeois civil order would ensure that wealth and status accrued to those with intelligence, industry and ability.

During the years 1789–92, the massive assault on birth, rank and privilege put the old order on the defensive. Titles were abolished. Offices were opened to talent. All were to be equally taxed. Equality before the law was established. Feudal dues were no longer enforced. The lord of the manor lost his judicial privileges over his peasants. Aristocrats were purged from the army and commissions became open to all classes. Tithes, internal customs tolls and fiscal immunities which had favoured Church and noble and lessened economic efficiency and well-being were eliminated, as were guilds and workers' associations. In 1791 the Civil Constitution of the Clergy nationalized Church properties, provided for the election of priests and bishops – who were to become paid civil servants – and made religious toleration official. The clergy were required to swear an oath of loyalty to the Civil Constitution. France was torn in two. The Pope condemned the Revolution. The King associated himself with the counter-revolution, sought to flee France and was later executed. France would now be ruled by a legislative assembly elected by those adult males who owned significant amounts of property. The Revolution moved further left. Aristocratic *émigrés* fled, and European conservatives began to look to their defences. Now they had to do battle with revolutionary and middle-class liberalism, not just with princes, and the new enemy promised to grow stronger with every step in the economic modernization of Europe.

EDMUND BURKE

Edmund Burke published his *Reflections on the Revolution in France* in October 1790; the work has remained ever since the most famous manifesto of the counter-revolution. Burke's heady rhetoric took conservatives by storm. The publication date shows that Burke's strictures were directed at the first or liberal phase of the Revolution, not at the radicalism of the Terror of 1792–94. Burke knew little, moreover, of the specific causes of the Revolution or of the events of 1789. He had developed many of his arguments previously as a leading politician and defender of the Whig oligarchy in England. His experience played him false. The English aristocracy, unlike the French, paid taxes, filled useful administrative posts and associated with and often joined in the more advanced economic projects of the middle classes. As for parliamentary government, the aristocracy had long been committed to it; indeed, Parliament had been their instrument since 1689.

Burke maintained that the great families of the landed aristocracy were the natural rulers of France. Were not they alone steeped in the ancient and time-tested social arrangements that accounted for the greatness of France? What other class possessed centuries of experience in the subtle intricacies of government? Sieyès notwithstanding, 200,000 men might well speak for 26 million, if they were the right 200,000. Burke chose to ignore or was not aware that the nobles of France, in their refusal to reform, represented no one but themselves. As for the King, Burke insisted – correctly as it turned out – that the National Assembly could not constitutionally limit the powers of the monarch without a struggle to the bitter end. Burke held it to be a contradiction in terms to limit a king; how would he receive the loyalty of his people if he could not command, reward and legislate without the permission of an elected assembly? George III, who is said to have admired Burke, would have read this wistfully indeed.

Burke detested the new rulers of France. His book is studded with uninformed insults against 'stock-jobbers', 'usurious Jews' and even 'assassins'. He says little that is specific about their deeds, preferring broad generalizations in spite of his conservative contempt for the 'metaphysicians' of the Enlightenment who spurned the realities of practical experience. Ignoring the extremely high percentage of civil servants and public magistrates in the Assembly, for example, Burke insisted that the latter was dominated solely by base representatives of the 'monied interests' who were by profession concerned only with immediate and private gain, and could thus have no sense either of the interests of the whole community or of the ageless values of a great nation. Such men viewed society as a mere business partnership for the material convenience of their own kind and their own generation. They were blind to the great truth: that society was a contract between not only the living, but the living, the dead and those who were yet to come. The new rulers of France, Burke held, mocked the wisdom of their ancestors and betrayed the trust of posterity. Radical change must always be wrong, because it could only be based on the transient interests, values and extremely narrow experience of a single generation.

Burke insisted that rights, like property, were inherited; he denounced those *philosophes* who, by endlessly prating about the rights of man, had encouraged the sheer destructiveness of the revolutionaries. Only through a wanton ignorance of reality had these inexperienced theoreticians arrived at the false doctrine of the equality of man. Instead of viewing society as it was, they had mentally stripped man of all his existing social functions and relationships, deprived him of his unique customs and historical traditions, and, finally, placed this lifeless abstraction in a fictional state of nature which they alleged was prior to all society and history. What else could result from this mathematician's delight except the claim that all men were equal, had the same rights and therefore the same right to rule? Was it any wonder, Burke asked, that every French hairdresser or shoemaker thought himself fit to vote on great affairs of state, and willingly partook in the destruction of the time-honoured institutions of the past – nobility, Church and Crown? Men should ignore idle speeches about natural rights and let centuries of experience and greatness be their guide. Their duty was to maintain and pass on to their heirs the political functions of each class and institution as they found them. The argument is circular, although Burke would never have admitted it. Had those ancient institutions functioned with such success, France in 1788 would hardly have been on the verge of bankruptcy and revolution.

Long before the Revolution, the Church had mounted a counter-offensive against the efforts of princes to secularize its wealth and limit its power. Theologians had also denounced the *philosophes'* critique of Christian dogmas. The *philosophes* were not atheists, but deists, arguing that there were a few religious truths which conformed to the observation of nature and the requirements of reason: God did exist; he had created the laws of nature and morality; and those who violated them would be punished. The rest, however, was mere superstition. At one stroke the rituals, dogmas and sacraments of the Church, as well as the unique claim of Catholicism to dispense divine grace, were peremptorily dismissed as the work of man, not God. Religious toleration and the separation of Church and state were justified. Moreover, deists saw God, in their famous phrase, as the 'Great Mathematician', who having once created the self-regulating laws of the universe, no longer interfered with its operations.

Conservative clerics were infuriated. Such notions deprived the ordinary man of the comfort of prayer, and also attacked the very foundations of Christianity: the ancient Christian miracles. Deists replied that if ancient texts spoke of men who observed the Red Sea divide or Christ rise from the dead, then it must be assumed that such testimony was fraudulent. The laws of evidence and reason dictated that this was much more probable than the suspension of the laws of nature by divine intervention. To this, Christian conservatives countered that the martyrdom of the ancient disciples proved their reliability, and that in any event finite human reason could not hope to judge God's infinite ways. Finally, must not a faith which had commanded the allegiance of both learned and unlearned for nearly 2,000 years be of necessity divine in origin? A warning was often added for the benefit of princes: their subjects would not obey if the faith which ordered work, suffering and humility were destroyed.

As we have seen, the Civil Constitution of the Clergy nationalized Church lands, reduced the number of benefices, enforced toleration and made the clergy elected and paid civil servants. In the debates of the Assembly, horrified conservatives insisted that a divine institution could only reform itself. How was it possible, for example, to take away the judicial powers of the Church when the Bible clearly stated that the Church must punish sinners? How could ordinary men, including followers of other faiths, be allowed to elect priests and bishops to holy office? The revolutionaries in the Assembly retorted that these measures in no way tampered with the spiritual essence of the faith, for they concerned only Church administration which had always been under the power of secular authorities. The more radical revolutionaries argued that the Church was part of the state, that the Pope himself was nothing but a foreign prince, and that his bishops – aristocrats to a man – were merely defending their own privileges, not the way of Christ. Such verbal and legislative assaults had their effects. By 1794 Mass was said in only a few hundred French parishes, and the Church hierarchy in France and all Europe had begun its role as a major bastion of ultra-conservative thought in the modern era.

Burke was not a Catholic, but he vehemently defended the rights of the French Church. The spirit of religion, he argued, held man's pride, lust and vicious appetites from tearing apart the social fabric. The social order as given was sacred in origin; man, tainted by original sin, could never change it for the better in any radical way. Fortunately, Burke added, man was religious by instinct and aware that he must one day account for his conduct to the great 'Author' of society. Burke scoffed at those eighteenth-century psychologists who, following Helvétius and Condillac, argued for social equality on the grounds that man possessed no innate qualities and derived his character and capacities from social and educational conditioning. With eighteenth-century conservatives before him, Burke held that man's social position from serf to noble was the consequence of God-given innate qualities intended to complement one another in a harmonious whole.

If the Jacobins broke the relationship between Church and state, Burke insisted, they would deprive public office and civic obligations of their divine sanction. When the Jacobins closed monasteries they destroyed institutions which contributed to public charity and men who set an ascetic model needed to remind all of their duty to combat the sins of the flesh. A wise statesman should not destroy useful institutions even if the latter had originated in superstition and failed to conform to the latest fads in science. Why, Burke asked, had the Jacobins not closed the brothels? As for electing priests and bishops, how would the truly meek and humble Christian ever survive the unprincipled search for votes? Deny the Church its wealth and power, Burke warned, and every barrier preventing a war of all against all would be removed. Evidently, Burke was not aware of the extent to which the French Church had itself become ridden with corruption.

5 'The knight of the woful countenance going to extirpate the National Assembly.' Armed with the shield of aristocracy and despotism, Burke rides into battle on the back of the Pope. Coloured engraving, November 1790.

In Burke's day, both liberals and conservatives thought history and society to be in some sense sacred in origin. Classical liberals, like Adam Smith, discerned beneficent, divine and natural laws governing the economic and social order; princes and parliaments needed only clear the way for everyone to follow his own rational self-interest, and these laws would automatically function to assure progress. From his conservative standpoint, Burke believed that God had incorporated a 'stupendous wisdom' in the instincts of the human race. Men ought to follow the ancient customs created by these instincts and avoid the 'feeble contrivances' of the conscious reasoning of social visionaries. The bounty of God, who favoured and protected the race of man, should not be abused. For Burke, sheer duration was ample testimony to the usefulness and practicality of institutions, class distinctions, laws and customs. Man's sacred heritage, Burke believed, would certainly need adjustments from time to time, but the wise statesman should make sure that he removed whatever seemed wrong only after ascertaining that greater wrongs would not ensue. At times, Burke implies that providence is responsible for all beneficial social change.

Conservatives claim that Burke was more sensitive to historical values than his liberal antagonists because he sought to judge the past on its own terms, while his opponents simply condemned it. Lacking the analytical tools of historical research developed in the nineteenth century, however, both Burke and his opponents tended to adopt conspiracy theories which were ahistorical by nature because they ascribed great social movements to the acts of a clever, ruthless few. The *philosophes* dismissed the medieval past as the corrupt product of thieving tyrants and superstitious priests, thus making their own values seem timeless, obvious and legitimate. Burke assumed that the vast majority of Frenchmen must have been content with the old régime. Therefore he argued that the Revolution was the result of the 'dark arts' of men like Voltaire, whose writings had filled the populace with a 'black and savage atrocity of mind' by wildly exaggerating the faults of nobles, priests and magistrates. Such destructive falsifications, Burke added, were financed by wealthy commoners jealous of noble status and prestige. Burke and other conservatives tended to accept such simplistic explanations, because otherwise they would have had to face the fact that a massive and successful upheaval like that of 1789 was in reality the result of deep and widespread discontent with the very institutions they admired. Burke's conspiracy theory led to his own solution: an armed intervention by *émigrés* and foreign armies who, he assumed, would easily destroy the tiny minority of revolutionaries and restore her traditional rulers to a grateful France.

How should societies be changed to meet the new needs of whose existence even Burke was aware? In 1789 there were no reliable statistics to define social realities, there was no franchise broad enough to reveal social discontent, and neither the tradition nor technology for anything remotely resembling social planning. It is not surprising that nearly all intellectuals, not only conservatives, avoided the issue by assuming that major social change was and ought to be – like the vast movement of the heavens themselves – the consequence of the laws of nature and of God. To paraphrase Burke: the statesman would look to the latent wisdom of inherited ways, and only with the greatest caution make the slightest adjustments, for there were no new discoveries to be made in the great principles of morality and society.

Burke saw no principles of even bourgeois social order in what he mistakenly regarded as an anarchistic drive for social equality. French leaders, he held, had ignored the principle basic to all social order: the action and counteraction of classes with different rights, powers and functions which limited the ability of any one group to dominate another and which established social harmony through mutual checks and balances. This, he insisted, was nature's way. The statesman needed only to negotiate careful compromises between competing groups. Social equality must bring social chaos and with it the terrible overcorrection of military despotism. Burke died before Napoleon's rise to power; he would not have been surprised by his success.

THE COUNTER-REVOLUTION

It is easy to understand the part played by aristocratic and clerical leaders of the old régime in the counter-revolution. Until recently, however, not enough attention has been paid to lower-class participation in the counter-revolution and conservative movements in general. In the 1790s in France nobles and clerics were able to muster sizeable Catholic and royalist forces from among artisans, peasants, day-labourers and the unemployed. These armed irregulars were at times strong enough to threaten the Revolution itself. Why would ordinary people fight to preserve the power and privileges of the well-born?

The resistance tended to come from the more backward areas of France. There, the liberal bourgeoisie and their reforming values had barely penetrated. Peasants produced for their own consumption; they had little access to the commercial, urban-centred market networks administered by bourgeois intermediaries. In backward areas, moreover, nobles tended to manage their own estates and perform traditional functions, retaining their former prestige. They were not so likely to lead idle lives in the cities, leaving their peasants to the mercies of estate managers. Traditional in their ways and with local concerns, peasants and artisans of the more remote districts remained stubbornly loyal to the old religion. The parish priest shared their poverty; he was the only transmitter of news and ideas from outside; and he filled many economic and political roles carried on elsewhere by the middle classes. When the revolutionaries harassed, deported and branded as traitors those priests who would not swear an oath of loyalty to the Civil Constitution of the Clergy, when they sent in priests as replacements, or when they seized Church properties to enforce administrative redistricting, they struck at the deepest emotional ties of rural villagers. Often thousands rose in protest to the cry of 'Long live the king and our good priest!'

Craftsmen and artisans in rural areas also often joined counter-revolutionary bands. The economic order of bourgeois free enterprise was a threat to the skilled textile workers who played a crucial part in the counter-revolutionary movements. In 1791 the revolutionaries had banned the guilds. Bourgeois cloth merchants controlled jobs and wages through their access to markets and raw materials. Before the Revolution textile workers and other craftsmen had rioted against the introduction of new machines which made their hard-won skills obsolete and their employment uneconomical. When craftsmen protested through normal channels, they met with the usual hypocrisy from government officials who consorted with important business interests. The view of those in power was that free enterprise would assure the well-being of all – in the long run.

When the peasants and artisans of the more remote districts of France were conscripted to defend the Revolution in 1793, it is not surprising that many took up arms in protest. What had the

Revolution achieved for them? Only the wealthy bourgeoisie could vote. It was usually the wealthy who benefited from the sale of Church lands, not the poorer peasants. Bourgeois and Jacobin local magistrates held a monopoly of public office, and could even keep their sons from battle by enrolling them in the National Guard. Deprived of their Church, their guilds and the sacred ways of their ancestors, the ordinary citizens of many backward regions adopted guerrilla tactics to fit their circumstances. Striking by surprise from hedge or window, they melted away after brief skirmishes. Concerned only with their own immediate districts, however, they could harass but not conquer; they had no way of permanently institutionalizing their values against the power of the Revolution. Still, they managed a sporadic resistance even under Napoleon, and throughout the nineteenth century they and similar groups helped to form a potential lower-class mass following for conservative social movements.

6 'Long live the king.' The portrait of Louis XVI is held up before an admiring crowd in a country farmhouse. Engraving by A. Legrand after Debucourt, 1789.

À tous FRANÇOIS bien nés , que -
cette IMAGE eſt chere .

III NAPOLEONIC IMPERIALISM AND THE CONSERVATIVE RESPONSE

Like European imperialism some three generations later, French imperialism under Napoleon posed grave threats to traditional values and pre-modern political, economic and social structures. The armies of the Republic and Napoleon routed those of other European régimes, and exposed the weakness of governments which could not command the loyalty of the bulk of their citizens. France was able to conscript masses of loyal citizens, collect huge sums in taxes, and field troops who fought with more skill, independence and spirit than the apathetic mercenaries and commandeered peasantry of her opponents. In the wake of his conquests, Napoleon brought most of the reforms of the Revolution with him; it was these reforms which had caused the ordinary Frenchman to identify his fate with that of his government.

While ending the self-government of the bourgeoisie in France, Napoleon consolidated all other liberal gains and exported them to his new empire. Where significant middle-class reform movements already existed, his reforms exerted a powerful impact. Throughout Europe his armies brought, with local variations, the first massive challenge to the established order. Where feasible, Napoleon abolished feudal dues and serfdom. Ruling princes and noble families were often deposed and replaced by local Jacobins or French bureaucrats. Aristocratic privileges were abolished and men were taxed according to wealth, not birth. Many vast estates were broken up or confiscated. Equality before the law was established. Offices were opened to talent, and feudal land-tenure systems were ended so that land could be purchased by the middle classes.

Although he once arrested the Pope and annexed the Papal States, Napoleon ultimately appeased the Church in France by compromise, because he wished to undercut the counter-revolution at home and the émigré bishops abroad. Nevertheless, Napoleon ruthlessly attacked the privileged position of the Church in the conquered territories. Church properties were seized, tithes and Church courts abolished, monasteries and convents suppressed, and divorce and religious toleration made legal. European conservatives were appalled when Napoleon opened ghettos and granted Jews freedom of worship and the right to own land and enter the trades. Moreover, he created lay institutions for public education and did his best to spread the ideas of the more moderate thinkers of the Enlightenment.

As a revolutionary 'enlightened despot' Napoleon eliminated many petty principalities and modernized the administration and economies of his satellite empire. Piecemeal princely jurisdictions and feudal particularism were replaced by general and codified regulations based on new French practice and enforced by professional bureaucrats. The latter created modern systems of accounting and taxation, initiated public works, including the building of roads, bridges and canals, and supervised the application of the latest scientific technology to agriculture. Before Napoleon's single-minded belief that all men should be ruled by the same laws, embodied in the great and influential *Code Napoléon*, feudal variations in customs and laws collapsed. Committed to the enterprising middle classes, Napoleon guaranteed the right to private property and the sanctity of business contracts. His economic advisers established modern banking and credit institutions and removed internal customs barriers to free trade.

On the other hand, Napoleon did little for those who were without land or wealth. He favoured the leading merchant and industrial families, and the kind of men who had dominated the Revolution before the Terror: magistrates, lawyers, property-owners and the professional classes in general. He supported the press, but censored it when it opposed him. In accord with his strong personal views, women's inferior status was legalized. Napoleon exploited his empire for France's economic advantage, conscripting the youth of other lands to fight in his campaigns. If he established constitutions and popularly elected assemblies, he rendered them powerless at any opposition. Nevertheless, Napoleon's threat to the established order was revolutionary and was felt to be so by the embattled leaders of Europe. In a manner typical of the dynamics of imperialism, his tyranny and his reforms generated both a wave of reform and a powerful defence of unique national traditions by threatened interests. Much that Napoleon built was destroyed after his defeat, but the memory lingered on, especially in the minds of the middle classes. The restored conservatives of the old régimes were increasingly forced to defend themselves ideologically and politically.

Before Napoleon's conquests, the rulers of the numerous petty states of the Germanies had little to fear from reformers. Excluding the Rhinelanders, the German middle classes tended to be dutiful civil servants or merchants and professional men who, if they accepted the liberalism of the Enlightenment, modified it in ways less critical of the establishment. Indeed, there was less to be critical about. Most of the larger states were well managed, and the aristocracy, especially in Prussia, were useful and hard-working servants of the state. Enlightened intellectuals, furthermore, felt no pressing need to attack the Church. The Lutheran clergy had little secular power, were obedient to the state and open to enlightened views. In fact, German intellectuals praised Lutheranism as the religion which accorded with the modern need for inner spiritual freedom, and scorned Catholicism as a worldly institution which insisted upon blind faith in outmoded dogmas and the efficacy of mindless ritual.

With one stroke Napoleon dissolved the feeble Holy Roman Empire and replaced its 300 separate political units by the 38 states of his Confederation of the Rhine. In the process he abolished the petty ecclesiastical states of the clergy and the tiny feudal fiefs of the imperial knights, against the protests of priests and canon lawyers using arguments we have already noted in the work of Justus Möser. Napoleon accomplished the greatest secularization of Church property since the Reformation, rewarding those German princes most likely to support his imperial designs with former clerical and feudal territories. There was no popular protest, for there was as yet little sense of national loyalty in Germany and what feeling there was found nothing to admire in these remnants of clerical power and feudal particularism. Indeed, before Napoleon's tyranny became obvious, significant numbers of citizens in western Germany welcomed French rule and even hoped for annexation.

Of all the European states, Prussia was to prove the most significant in the history of European conservatism. Prussia unified Germany in the late nineteenth century under the leadership of ultra-conservatives presiding over an unprecedented industrial revolution. Conservative institutions and ideas, as we shall see, were thus given a mighty power base at the onset of the present century. In 1807, however, Prussia existed only at the pleasure of Napoleon and at the cost of the surrender of much territory, population and treasure. From this humiliation emerged the call for liberal reform. Led by Baron vom Stein, Prince Hardenberg and Generals Gneisenau and Scharnhorst, the younger members of the Prussian bureaucratic and military establishment sought to tap the national energies of their people by a revolution from above. Serfs were freed so that they might become efficient farmers and grateful citizens. The coercive powers of the guilds were ended to stimulate the spirit of free enterprise. The rigid Prussian caste system was eased, with all offices, even military ones, declared open to talent rather than birth. Public education was initiated, and some self-government was granted. The King, Frederick William III, even promised that one day these reforms would be incorporated in a constitution representing all classes.

Prussian conservatives were horrified, and the objections of the nobles were presented in a memorandum to the King. The author of this document, Friedrich von der Marwitz, was himself a Junker army officer. Like his fellow nobles, Marwitz found all such reforms French, un-Prussian and alien. If Prussia's citizens had not fought well for her, he argued, it was not because they lacked any fictitious rights of man. It was because Prussian institutions had been weakened when Frederick the Great humbled the nobility and governed without their consent. Imported French liberalism, Marwitz added, would only further erode the cohesion of the Prussian community spirit by preaching selfish individualism and materialism. Prussia was a patriarchal state based, as it should be, on the model of the family. To free the serfs, Marwitz insisted, was to deprive them of the genuine concern of the lord of the manor, to attack the property rights of the nobles and to sanctify rootless 'freedom' at the expense of social stability. Drawing upon arguments presented by Christian Garve, a well-known conservative thinker of the time, Marwitz held that serfs were in any case a separate and conquered race – by nature stupid and lazy. Freeing or educating the serf would make him discontented with his lot and unfit for productive service on the manor or for hard military training on the drill-ground. The reformers, Marwitz continued, insisted that free enterprise must be introduced for the sake of efficiency, but if the established system of guild controls were destroyed, would not the Prussian sense of community be further weakened by the ensuing unlimited and destructive competition between individuals? Marwitz also advised the King not to allow the reformers to break up noble estates, for to do so would be to undermine the very class responsible for Prussia's greatness.

Prussian conservatives of all classes were shocked by proposals to emancipate the Jews. Drawing on ideas already old in the Germanies, Marwitz insisted that the Jews were a ruined race, doomed by the Almighty to wander forever, incapable of loyalty to any state and unfit to labour as honest peasants or fighting men. Jews must not be allowed to purchase land, because this would deliver Prussia into the hands of greedy 'stock-jobbers' and 'old and honourable Prussia would become a new-fangled Jew-state'. To those reformers who suggested the liberation of women, Marwitz retorted that women were obviously born domestics whose spirit could never rise above the care of children, the joys of sex and the petty concerns of gossip. Women were the mainstay of family life. Was it not sufficient for them to raise, comfort and nurse the dominant male? Tradition and right, Marwitz concluded, declared that political power belonged to nobles and princes; all others must perform their traditional functions. It was typical of conservatives, threatened by invasion and reform, to respond by calling for a revival of strength through a return to the unsullied principles of the past.

Nevertheless, the sheer power of Napoleon gave the reformers a temporary ascendancy at the Prussian court. The King and his former advisers detested the values of the French Enlightenment, and were adherents of the mystical and counter-revolutionary order of the Rosicrucians. The Rosicrucians made no concessions to Newtonian science: for them the Bible was literally true; alchemy and astrology were exact sciences. The courtiers surrounding the King speculated endlessly about the secret of perpetual youth and the raising of the dead. According to the Rosicrucians, the catechism was all that was needed by the masses. The Revolution was simply the result of the plotting of Freemasons. In all things one owed perfect obedience to God, and on earth this meant perfect obedience to one's divinely established worldly superiors. It was a philosophy fit for a king.

The defeat of Napoleon halted Prussian reforms. Serfs were freed, but were forced to pay so much in compensation to their former lords that the wealth and lands of the nobles increased along with the indebtedness of the peasantry. Guild powers were restored, Jews were not emancipated and women remained in their traditional roles. The King, an admirer of medieval institutions, allowed no constitution,

7 Contemporary caricature of loyal German supporters of Napoleon on hearing the news of his surrender, 15 July 1815. Goethe, who had identified Napoleon as the saviour of European civilization, is seated on the far right.

although he did make concessions to the heavily propertied upper bourgeoisie in the restored and largely ceremonial noble diets. The Napoleonic experience forced certain military changes. Some men of common birth were given commissions, and officers were instructed to forego entering battle followed by huge wagon-trains filled with personal luxury items. But no attempt was made to create the citizen army desired by the more radical reformers. The King and his advisers feared civilian influence on the army, the bulwark of reaction. The wars of liberation against Napoleon had been won by the professional troops of Austria and Prussia; there was no longer any need to seek strength in citizen soldiers. The police were ordered to exile or imprison the remaining members of the 'international liberal conspiracy', and rioting protesters were suppressed with ease and pleasure. In spite of Napoleon, Prussia continued to be ruled by Hohenzollerns, their noble bureaucratic chiefs and military commanders. Elsewhere in the Germanies, except to some degree in the south-west, liberal constitutions were abrogated and the old institutions remained intact.

Until the 1860s, the Austrian Empire controlled and set the standards for the ideas and practices of the counter-revolution in Europe, because it was in the Empire that the ideal conditions for the reign of ultra-conservatism were to be found. Enlightened despotism had failed; the landed aristocracy dominated the far-flung imperial bureaucracy; the bourgeoisie was small and without influence; the guilds were unchallenged; the Church retained all of its powers – while only their economic usefulness kept the Jews from being banished outright from Vienna and Prague. To mobilize opinion against Napoleon, imperial officials had promised liberal reforms, but such gestures were abandoned after repeated defeats cost the Empire extensive territories and population.

The Emperor, Francis II, preferred to change nothing. As far as reforms for the masses were concerned, he believed in the old aristocratic slogan, 'The human race begins with barons.' His favourite pleasure was to read the reports of his police spies. Like the Jesuits and nobles who surrounded him at court, he feared science, industrialization and the introduction of railways, because these created middle-class liberals, subversive intellectuals and popular unrest. He once punished a delegation of peasants who, representing starving fellow villagers, humbly petitioned for lower wheat tariffs. He forbade his ministers to arouse national loyalties against Napoleon among the diverse ethnic groups of the Empire. He sensed that, whatever the short-term gains, no concessions could be made to liberalism and nationalism in multi-national, feudal empires like Austria's, where national consciousness and self-determination would mean eventual dissolution.

After Napoleon defeated the Austrian armies at Wagram in 1809, Francis II turned to Count Klemens von Metternich as the man most able to preserve the Empire from Napoleon by diplomatic manoeuvre, and from liberalism by repression. Born to wealth and title, Metternich, who was to be made a prince in reward for his services, saw his family estates confiscated by French armies. He had the perfect temperament for diplomacy: he believed in nothing, took no statement at face value and avoided all commitments until certain of the winning side. He paid conservative intellectuals to mobilize conservative opinion among the articulate élites, who otherwise might not see where their true interests lay; but he declined to disturb the masses. His secretary and chief propagandist, Friedrich von Gentz, was a devoted reader of Justus Möser and the translator of Edmund Burke. Gentz hoped to create a theory of counter-revolution to stem the tide of liberalism; Metternich was prepared to settle for an acceptable defence of imperial institutions.

Typically, Metternich's major theoretical statement was in the form of a personal memorandum to Tsar Alexander I who, to Metternich's consternation, had toyed with the dangerous notion of making liberal reforms in his multi-national empire. Appealing to the Tsar's well-known sense of religion, Metternich argued that the roots of the French Revolution were to be found in the arrogance of the leaders of the Protestant Reformation, who had challenged the true Church and thus established a precedent for the contemporary fury of the middle classes against all divinely established institutions and class distinctions. Liberalism was a heresy and a disease. Consequently, no compromises could be made; its supporters must be silenced.

It is hardly surprising that in Austria, as in Russia, economic growth was discouraged, especially as its relationship to military power had not yet been demonstrated. In Austria internal tariffs were maintained, railroad-building was held back, capital was diverted from middle-class hands, guilds were strengthened and industries were required to build away from urban centres of potential unrest.

The landed aristocracy of Austria were the most caste-conscious in Europe and had nothing but contempt for the middle classes. Princess Metternich herself demonstrated this when at a charity ball in Vienna she erected a card-table barrier to separate aristocrats from even the most select of the upper bourgeoisie. Liberal reforms frightened the Austrian aristocracy; more than other European élites, they depended on the long hours, forced labour and innumerable obligations of their serfs to support a luxurious and highly ceremonial life of leisure. They were joined in their fears by the most reactionary Church in Europe, whose clergy obsessively denounced 'atheistic' liberalism from the pulpit. The higher clergy also led the campaign against the emancipation of the Jews, who were not only the symbols of the antichrist, but tended to be enlightened liberals. The government prevented Jews from owning land, working as civil servants and participating in a variety of trades and professions. Special permits were required for Jews who wished to live or work in Vienna.

Without the benefit of sophisticated theories of social change, the Austrian élites simply transformed their fears into an erroneous belief that liberalism and nationalism had great potential power in the Empire. But only economic modernization could create a significant liberal bourgeoisie and uproot the Slav peasantry from their local loyalties and kinship ties. Liberalism in Austria was confined to a handful of intellectuals in one or two urban centres. Nationalism was as yet limited to a tiny group of pioneering literati, creating the native literatures and discovering the unique histories of their particular ethnic groups. Metternich's repressive measures, therefore, were not only unnecessary but were too feeble to be effective had the threats been real. Newspapers were government-controlled; police spies were used so extensively that even Metternich's own mail was opened; thousands were arrested on mere suspicion of liberal views; the very word 'constitution' was banned; students were not allowed to study abroad; professors were told in detail what to teach; and the Church was given strict control over censorship and education. The Empire remained, as the popular phrase had it, 'a standing army of soldiers, a sitting army of bureaucrats, a kneeling army of priests and a crawling army of serfs'.

THE HOLY ALLIANCE

When Napoleon was finally defeated, the leaders of Prussia, Russia and Austria used the Congress of Vienna (1815) to make the world safe for conservatism. They formed a Holy Alliance to suppress those liberals and nationalists still active in secret societies and to restore the principles of the old order. The Congress has often been praised for the long duration of its peace settlements, but it ought to be noted that until nationalism and liberalism became truly powerful forces their influence was easily contained by the professional armies of the conservative régimes. The greatest danger was neutralized·from the start when Metternich and the allied leaders cautioned the restored Louis XVIII not to reverse all the moderate revolutionary gains of 1789–91 for fear of stimulating mass uprisings in France. Elsewhere the old ways and dynasties were re-established, modified only by the victors' desire to reward and compensate each other by exchanging peoples (without their consent) and to restore their European empires. This could still be done with little trouble in the east and south where, outside of the major urban networks, peasants kept their local loyalties and perceived no striking variations in the rule of different feudal monarchs.

The conservative principle of maintaining the balance of power through territorial exchanges rested on this lack of mass participation; it no longer worked when popular nationalism and ethnic consciousness swept Europe later in the century, making such transfers of populations extremely difficult. The Congress of Vienna gave Austria parts of Italy. Russia gained Finland. Prussia received considerable accretions of territory in Germany. All three powers, as usual, took shares of Poland. Belgium was given to the Dutch, but Belgium was economically, *per capita*, the most advanced European state and contained a highly politicized population. Here conservative principles were bound to fail, and Belgium gained its independence in 1830. In Italy and Spain there were minor revolts in the 1820s, led by professional groups, ex-officers of Napoleon's armies, some lesser nobles and elements of the commercial middle classes. But the Holy Alliance was able to crush such revolts with ease and brutality, as they had little popular support. Declaring that they were guided by God, the allied princes insisted upon their right to invade any European state where revolutionary movements pitted a 'mistaken' people against the legitimate prince.

Excluding France, there was no overwhelming opposition to the restoration of the old order. In Spain the arch-reactionary Ferdinand VII ended all legislative traces of the revolutionary era, although initial difficulties caused him to shoot thousands out of hand. In the Kingdom of the Two Sicilies there was very little objection to the return to 1788. The Kingdom was overwhelmingly agrarian, and its peasants, illiterate and plague-ridden, still used hand flails and wooden ploughs. The Vatican regained its Papal States, restored the Society of Jesus and ended all talk of a free and united Italy. More new and counter-revolutionary religious orders were founded during these years than by any generation since the thirteenth century. Throughout Italy both Church and manorial powers were restored, commoners were denied high office, Napoleonic legislation was stricken from the books, and tens of thousands of civil servants and military officers were purged – to be replaced by Slavs and Germans, immune to either liberalism or Italian nationalism. Censorship suppressed dangerous books, especially those, like the works of Jeremy Bentham and the British liberals, which insisted that government existed to provide the greatest good for the greatest number. The study of Italian history was discouraged. Metternich hoped that Italy (and Germany) would remain no more than geographical expressions.

The revolutionary era had made nationalism into a force working for liberalism as well. Moreover, should Italy be united, the Austrian Empire might be driven from southern Europe. Should Germany be united, Austrian dominance in central Europe would end. Although Metternich knew this, he did not know that he had little to fear. Nationalism in Italy had an extremely narrow social base; in the Germanies it was supported only by a few articulate but politically insignificant students and university professors. Yet in the midst of the revolutionary era there were no certain guidelines for those who hoped either to prevent or to provoke social upheavals. Like so many of his contemporaries, Metternich greatly overestimated the power of the written word and the ideas of a few.

Together with the leading princes of the Germanies, Metternich took appropriate preventive measures in the Carlsbad Decrees of 1819. Their declared purpose was to maintain peace, property and the old social order by silencing the 'pernicious' and 'subversive' voices of liberal nationalists. Each university was assigned a government representative whose task was to fire and blacklist all instructors, expel all students and ban all secret societies of liberal persuasion. Press and publication were placed under strict censorship, and a Central Investigating Commission was set up to harass any potentially dangerous groups or individuals. It became extremely difficult to publish liberal ideas in central Europe for the next twenty years. But, increasingly, conservatives became aware that they would have to do more than simply take defensive measures. The rising tide of liberalism demanded that conservatives defend the old order by ideological statements directed at the literate public, combined with political action. Organizations of aristocrats, lay religious groups and guildsmen flourished, and men of high birth moved swiftly to monopolize crucial positions in government, court, army, Church and the diplomatic corps.

IV CONSERVATISM IN THE ROMANTIC AGE

The mighty social upheavals of 1789–1815 were unprecedented, unplanned and unforeseen. The generation which lived through these bewildering transformations was the first truly lost generation of modern Europe. Men were rudely thrust from the predictable world of their ancestors, often stripped of their identity, and, excluding the peasant masses, found themselves unable to enjoy what Metternich defined as freedom – the certainty that tomorrow would always be exactly the same as today. During the revolutionary years princes were exiled; nobles became homeless commoners; monks, nuns and priests were exiled or forced to renounce their orders; petty states disappeared from the map; young men were torn from the villages of their ancestors and launched at distant armies in foreign lands; an unknown Corsican became emperor of France and half of Europe, while old laws and institutions crumbled before his sword. To paraphrase Alfred de Musset, a profound interpreter of the feelings of his own generation: when the youth of the revolutionary era looked behind them in 1815, they saw only the ruins of centuries of absolutism; when they looked about them they saw only the uneasy, restored fossils of a discredited past; ahead of them they saw a future full of uncertainty, where anything seemed possible.

Out of these contradictory tensions came that burst of creative energy which has labelled the first half of the nineteenth century the age of Romanticism and ideology. The remnants of the past created both nostalgia and contempt. The confusing changes of the present brought a frustrated search for that which was worth preserving, and a glorification of the self when all else seemed transient. The sense of unlimited possibilities brought with it anxiety, hope and a dramatic awareness of the need to create a new world to replace the old. It is not surprising that from 1789 to 1850 almost every major ideology of modern Europe was born.

In art, literature and poetry, the revolutionary generation sought the forms and subjects to communicate new experiences and more intense emotions. In social theory and philosophy, new evolutionary concepts replaced the static and mechanistic thinking of Newton and

the *philosophes*. Now, like the most important philosopher of the age, Hegel, one strove to comprehend the dialectical relationships between the real and the ideal, matter and spirit, dead reality and living thought. Long before Darwinism, this generation was forced by its revolutionary trauma to think in terms of change, growth and evolution, because it was the first to witness them on a grand scale.

These were decades, in short, which demanded ideological solutions and even Utopian visions of what society ought to be. In a period of upheaval, conquest and defeat, with ever-changing laws, institutions and constitutions, it would have been impractical not to project the fears and hopes for social and cultural reconstruction into theories potentially capable of realization. Only much later would the complex dynamics of social change be more clearly understood.

8–10   Varieties of Romantic nostalgia. Opposite: left, the heroic age: illustration to Ossian (Fingal), by Philip Otto Runge, 1805–6; right, the medieval setting: 'Winter', calendar page by Theodor Rehbenitz, 1818. Above, the ruins of the past: *The Dreamer*, by Caspar David Friedrich, 1820–25.

Utopian thinking has often been identified exclusively by both left and right with Utopian socialism. Wishing to preserve their image of caution and pragmatism as opposed to the visionaries of the left, conservatives have denied their own Utopian intellectual heritage. Yet many well-known conservative theorists idealized the medieval past as a sacred, intricate and balanced social order, and as an alternative to urban and industrial sameness, the 'dark Satanic mills' and escalating dissatisfaction with a materialistic society. Many on the right found their nostalgia for an age of faith, chivalry and heroic nobility expressed in the immensely popular novels of Sir Walter Scott. Others sought to revive the once despised art and architecture of the Middle Ages. Long-neglected ruins were restored or maintained in magnificent decay – stark, lonely and emotion-laden symbols of the desolation traditionalists felt when they contemplated the world Europe had lost. Many conservative intellectuals deserted the cold and graceless axioms of deism and Protestantism to convert to Catholicism with its glorious past, its aesthetic genius, its heady rituals and the infinite mysteries of its divine grace. After the Revolution, conservatives of all classes sensed the intricate relationship between their concerns and those of the Catholic Church, and behaved accordingly.

One of the most influential advocates of the imagined social principles of the Middle Ages was the poet Novalis. In his *Christenheit Oder Europa?* (1799) Novalis praised the 'splendid days' when Europe had been not just a collection of warring nations, but one vast political and moral empire of the spirit, under the holy leadership of the Pope: the wise, disinterested counsellor of princes. Under the guidance of a universally respected priestly guild, all men had found comfort and forgiveness for their sins. The cold uncertainties of secular reason, Novalis believed, had not then eroded man's childlike faith and taught him that the universe was an alien machine, indifferent to human needs and unable to echo his moral values or yield solace for the day's frustrations. Was it not wise of the Holy Pontiff, Novalis asked, to prevent scientists from announcing their dangerous knowledge and discoveries? Should men really learn despair from Galileo by conceiving of the earth not as the centre of the drama of salvation, but as a ball of mud revolving round a third-rate star?

Teach men to reject the essential sacredness of the universe, Novalis warned, and they would turn on their planet and each other, destroying the balance of nature and man in endless battles of greed and lust. The harmony of medieval society in which each class had contentedly performed its duties and enjoyed its rights, secure in the knowledge that its social functions were divinely sanctioned and would be divinely rewarded, had been replaced by mere love of gain and commerce. The result was an endless search to fill the spiritual void with material comforts. Thus the ideal bond of Christian spirituality had been broken; it was the duty of Europeans to restore it.

Novalis's Romantic vision of a regained medieval spirituality was revived again and again by religious traditionalists, men frightened and appalled by the decline of other-worldliness, the erosion of ideal values and the rise of the raw, crude and raucous vitality of urban industrialism.

ADAM MÜLLER

It was Adam Müller who, in 1809, published the most profound statement of conservative political principles to emerge from the Romantic era: *Die Elemente der Staatskunst*. The work surpassed even that of Burke. It established Müller as a favourite of the Austrian court, and brought him stipends and posts to enable him, urged on by his protector Metternich, to defend the Empire against the clamour for reform. The *Elemente* originated, appropriately enough, as a series of lectures given to an audience of princes, aristocrats and diplomats in the year Metternich was appointed Austrian chancellor.

Müller's major theme was clear and direct. Only a return to medieval principles of government could restore Austria's greatness. Prussia and Austria had declined because even their feudal élites had succumbed to the selfish spirit of liberal individualism. They had forgotten what feudal warriors understood: that society was a community based on mutual sacrifice for the perpetual struggle against nature and foreign intrusion. War and the collective spirit of war, Müller argued, must be incorporated in all state institutions. Only thus would men be constantly reminded of their dependence upon each other, and realize that their fate was bound up unalterably with that of the community.

The organic unity of medieval society, Müller observed, had been destroyed in France and Europe long before Napoleon. Why then was Napoleonic liberalism so powerful militarily? Because Napoleon countered liberal individualism with the use of police terror to hold together the shattered remnants of a once truly corporate state. In Müller's view, only despots believed that territories and peoples could simply be merged like mathematical units, completely disregarding their unique characteristics. Napoleon's liberal reforms were actually intended to increase his personal power. It seemed just, Müller pointed out, to deprive the nobles of their extraordinary powers and wealth. But in reality this deprived the community of a class capable of resisting Napoleonic tyranny. All citizens might become equal, but they also became equally powerless. Müller insisted that the collapse of Napoleon's empire was inevitable, for his drastic transformations would finally serve to awaken in all conquered peoples a strong sense of their own national identities. Needless to say, Metternich gave Müller no policy-making position in his own empire of diverse peoples.

Like many Romantics, Müller hoped that man's yearnings for the ideal could be embodied in the actual social arrangement of his various distinctive cultures. But Müller argued that for generations there had been a steady deterioration of those vital ideal values which, under the medieval Church, had infused institutions, corporate bodies and individuals with the Christian spirit of mutual trust and sacrifice for the good of the whole. Protestantism had made religion a merely private matter for the individual conscience; princes had torn away the properties and powers of the Church; and secular intellectuals had scorned its ancient truths. All had ignored the fact that it was the Church which had performed the mighty task of founding Europe when it civilized the barbarian hordes; and it was the Church, too, which had always held up the spirit of righteousness to sinning man. Deprived of the power to make real the divine spirit, was it any wonder that modern society was given over to the war of all against all sanctioned by bourgeois liberalism? By their commitment to private property and individual rights, liberals were the natural enemies of true communities. Liberalism resulted in alienated individuals who, lacking a powerful and institutionalized Christianity, could only be forced into cooperative efforts through Napoleonic terror or enlightened despotism. Even the Church hierarchy itself, long before Napoleon, had surrendered to cynicism and material gain by treating its rights and prerogatives in the manner of a common, greedy merchant. Together with other Romantic conservatives, Müller was never simply a defender of the *status quo*, but an idealistic social visionary hoping to restore to society its medieval sense of mission.

Müller was thus a reactionary, although one hesitates to use a term so unjustly reviled by liberal historians and even conservatives, who perhaps fear guilt by association. Whatever one thinks of Müller's highly idealized vision of medieval institutions, he was no simple defender of the crude material interests of the nobility, as was Marwitz. Müller did agree that noble landowners should have their property, status and monopoly of high office protected by law. For only thus, he thought, could the families of ancient lineage fulfil their feudal trust and the community's debt to the dead by transmitting to posterity their ancient estates and customs as living symbols of honoured traditions. Unfortunately, Müller added, the aristocracy of Europe, like the noble parasites of France, had increasingly treated their exalted position as a right without obligations and had thus aided the destruction of the community spirit. If the nobles continued to treat the lands in their trust as mere property to be exploited, the counter-revolution would not succeed. The clergy and the aristocracy were both partly responsible for the Revolution, because they had deserted the social morality of medieval and feudal Christianity and had absorbed the spirit of liberal individualism. Learn from the fate of ancient Israel, Müller admonished, whose national community was destroyed when the Jews murdered Christ.

Müller found the major source of contemporary immorality in the liberal doctrine which held that the state was a convenient device invented by men in order to preserve the rights possessed in some imagined prior state of nature. Thus liberals prefaced their constitutions with declarations of the allegedly inalienable and natural rights of man, and seriously contended that individuals might enter, leave, or even revolt against society should they feel those rights to have been violated. Was it not obvious, Müller asked, that men were nowhere to be found born alone into this mythical state of nature? Man was always and everywhere born into some actual form of social relationship – family, tribe, clan or nation – and his rights and functions were derived from this living relationship. Liberals falsely assumed that each society must be rebuilt according to abstract laws of reason. In so doing they destroyed the historically created values of the past, and encouraged both the anarchy of Robespierre and the tyranny of Napoleon.

Like all Romantics, Müller believed in the existence of a transcendental realm of ideal values, which should and did modify man's political and social behaviour. But liberals erred when they assumed that these ideal values could be expressed in a fixed and final list of the rights of man. From the beginning of time men had sought to create a moral order, but one conditioned by a variety of different social situations. The enlightened thinkers of France and their middle-class supporters had illegitimately transformed their transient material interests into so-called eternal dictates of nature and reason, thus giving alienated individualism and commercial avarice a false universal sanction. The social contract so prized in liberal thought, Müller argued, was an agreement representing the needs of only one class, which, by emphasizing the inviolability of individual rights, limited forever the power of the community to control its own fate. In reality, all living societies were contracts between the needs and functions of different groups; all were the result of compromise between man's ideal yearnings and his material needs.

The only way to restore harmony, Müller insisted, was to look upon the state, as medieval man had, not as an aggregate of individuals but as a community of communities in which every citizen was part of a lesser community – nobles, priests, guildsmen, merchants – each with as much power of self-regulation as was consistent with its function and the good of the whole. In such a social order the only conflicts would be between corporate groups strong enough to maintain their particular functions; no one group would be able to usurp functions unnatural to its calling and ride roughshod over the rest. Thus the age-old struggle between the modernizing merchant and the conservative guildsman would yield the correct balance between tradition and innovation, just as the conflicting interests of prince, noble and priest would limit the self-aggrandizement of each order and contribute to the harmony of the whole. As in medieval times, a series of mediating figures and institutions would emerge to maintain justice and settle disputes between groups: the monarchy; the guildmasters; the urban patriciate; and the basic and most natural organic unit, the patriarchal family. There would be neither place nor need for the anti-social and all-powerful self-concern of the individual.

According to classical economic theory, if each followed his rational self-interest the good of the whole would automatically result. This, in Müller's view, was a destructive attack on the 'immortal state-family' for the advantage of one particular group: the merchants and entrepreneurs. The so-called natural laws of economics, he argued, were actually crude abstractions from exceedingly complex interrelationships between economic and non-economic factors; the function of these laws was to allow the propertied bourgeoisie to rid themselves of their social conscience and deny responsibility for their acts. The state must view all its works, institutions, capital and cultural products as the precious, stored-up energies of generations. No single class, but the community as a whole, must guide and regulate production, distribution and credit. Why should the private money-lender be allowed to foreclose the honest peasant? Why should the guilds go under to mass producers of shoddy goods? Why should imported goods be allowed to break the sacred bond between a people and the unique products of their own craft and soil?

In 1809, Müller could hardly have foreseen the mighty power that the community-shattering bourgeoisie were to give to those states that encouraged free enterprise during the coming age of coal, steam and steel. For Müller and his fellow conservatives, strength seemed to lie in the psychological and collective unity of the community. Moreover, Müller was too narrowly concerned with the divisive effects of liberal individualism, and ignored the strength to be gained by liberal reforms which caused great numbers of the productive classes to identify their fate with that of the government and state. Such reforms would, in any case, be anathema to the rulers of the Austrian Empire, for they would merely add to the forces of ethnic diversity threatening German and Habsburg dominance.

THE RESTORATION

The Bolshevik revolution of 1917 destroyed or exiled the privileged classes, and created the basis for a monolithic society. But in France and Europe in 1815 the old rulers regained power, and the stage was set for the complex class confrontations of the nineteenth century. Returning élites in France purged Bonapartists, Jacobins and liberals, taking their cue from the words of the brilliant conservative, Chateaubriand: 'A bishop, an army-commander, a prefect, a police chief; if these are for God and king, I will answer for the rest.' All was restored, yet all was changed. Now monarchs must fear their subjects, lords their peasants, priests their parishioners, and employers their workers. Throughout Europe the response was repression and a successful return to the nobles' monopoly of high office in government, Church and army. The Church regained many of its former powers. Even the living standards of the aristocrats suffered little. But for the rest of the century conservatives would have to fight a constant rearguard action against the bourgeoisie and the working classes, both increasing in number and political consciousness with each decade.

In France the immediate campaign to reverse the results of the revolutionary era was mounted by the returning former *émigré* aristocrats. The ultra-royalists or 'ultras', as they came to be called, were returned by force of allied arms to reign over an apathetic, potentially dangerous, but war-weary France. Among the returning exiles were the two most influential theorists of the reaction in France, the Comte de Maistre and the Vicomte de Bonald. Born a member of the Sardinian nobility, de Maistre had seen his estates occupied by the French. De Maistre's sovereign, the Duke of Savoy, appointed him, appropriately enough, as representative to the court of the Tsar. There de Maistre composed the work that was to have the most influence on the ultra-royalists of France, his *Considérations sur la France* of 1796.

De Maistre's work was far more theological and reactionary than that of Burke or even Müller. He made no concessions whatsoever to the ability of conscious human reasoning to create anything that was worthwhile or lasting. As he put it, if the puny intellect of man could not even create an insect, how could it claim to fashion a lasting social and moral order? The legislation of Moses and the divinely ordained institutions of the Vatican had lasted; but what had been the fate of the many constitutions and laws of the revolutionaries? The will of God, not the reason of man, had generated all lasting laws, institutions and societies. In de Maistre's view, if men desired a stable and just social order they should write no constitutions, invent no laws, but follow instead the divinely implanted instincts of the bulk of mankind – instincts which informed them that it was best to do things as they had always been done. Did fathers and children have need of constitutions to tell them how to behave towards one another? Were not the intricate emotional relationships of the family – the model of all social order – the result of arrangements whose divine origins must always remain a mystery to even the most enlightened of thinkers?

For de Maistre, all true government was sustained by divine miracles; no nation could possibly give itself a legitimate constitution. What rational being would base his choice of monarch on the blind accidents of heredity? Yet, de Maistre continued, was this not precisely the form of government that had lasted longest in Europe? As for the rights of man, it followed that one could only claim those rights that one's class had always possessed. De Maistre admitted that there were a multitude of social ills, but the social order as given was balanced. To correct one abuse was to create another. Even if it were agreed that nobles should not inherit office, was it really an improvement if office-holders were appointed by the votes of the ignorant masses instead? Granted, imperialism was bloody; but did it not also create civilized men out of savages? Even as de Maistre wrote, the priests and soldiers of France had already begun their long adventure of Christianizing and 'civilizing' Indochina.

But if social arrangements were the result of divine providence, how then could one account for the Revolution and Napoleon? Unlike Burke, de Maistre did not avoid the issue with feeble conspiracy theories. For him, Robespierre and Napoleon were instruments of the divine wrath of God. The altruistic revolutionaries and God-haters of the eighteenth century had destroyed God's institutions, proclaiming that human reason alone should rule. So be it, God had declared: once and for all men should see the brutal and bloody consequences of the reign of antichrist. Let God's monsters, the Jacobins, purify Europe by purges. According to de Maistre, the Revolution itself was a divine miracle. Conservatives must not put themselves above God by hoping to end it before it had run its full course; the masses would then always lament the loss of what they thought their abortive revolution might have achieved. But once the scourge had destroyed itself, the terrorized populace would heave a vast sigh of relief at the return of king, Church and aristocracy. All would be purified, in fact: princes would no longer toy with reform, nobles would no longer read Voltaire, and the clergy would cleanse themselves of their recently adopted worldly cynicism.

De Maistre was not disturbed by the thought that millions of innocent people were suffering at the hands of the Jacobins. If the innocent never suffered undeserved pain and if the guilty were always punished for their crimes, he argued, there would be no moral order. Moral choices must always be accompanied by unpredictable consequences or they would not be free choices, but simply conditioned reflexes. More than any other Catholic conservative thinker, de Maistre was convinced that most men would choose evil most of the time. Thus his ultimate paradox: the living symbol of divine providence was the state executioner. Remove the man whose very profession it was to do evil, and thrones, laws and the social order itself would collapse. When the old rulers of Savoy returned to power it is not surprising that they appointed de Maistre as head of the judiciary. In his later writings, de Maistre drew the logical conclusion of his contempt for human arrangements. Even the princes of Europe should have no final authority: the Pope must be Europe's law-giver.

The Vicomte de Bonald shared de Maistre's view that every good society must be a theocracy. Bonald, however, was a practising politician. Elected to France's most reactionary Chamber of Deputies ever, that of 1815, he could hardly wait for divine providence to restore the sacred order. Bonald supported the ultras' attempt to restore lands and powers to Church and noble and keep the professional and commercial bourgeoisie from power. He personally led the ultras as they made divorce illegal, sacrilege punishable by death, and used rigid censorship to instruct the 'violent and ignorant' public in the traditional principles of social order.

In spite of de Maistre, conservatives had to work through an elected Chamber of Deputies until they felt strong enough to overthrow it. Thus Bonald's thought has a more modern ring, if only because of his need to listen to the arguments of his opponents in order to outmanoeuvre them. He enjoyed noting in the presence of liberals that though they castigated the harsh feudal régimes of the past, it was the France of the Rights of Man that had extinguished the rights of Europe. He stressed the destructive effects of modern industrialism as well. Who was the real enemy of the ordinary worker, Bonald asked, the guild master training his apprentices in his own household, or the bourgeois employer who, proclaiming the freedom and dignity of labour, proceeded to render the worker helpless by outlawing his guilds, so that he might exploit without limit all those whose careful skills he had replaced by the mindless rhythms of the machine? Having lost any pleasure in skilled achievement, the worker under the new order faced the prospect of being easily replaced by avaricious

LA CLÉ D'OR

OUVRANT LES TRÉSORS DU CRÉDIT ET DE LA LIBERTE, FERMANT LA PORTE A LA BANQUEROUTE.

11 'The Golden Key – opening the treasury of credit and liberty, closing the door to bankruptcy.' A village elder expounds the virtues of self-help, thrift and hard work to a group of villagers. Coloured woodcut, Metz 1835–40. Broadsheets such as this, based on the *Poor Richard's Almanack* of Benjamin Franklin (1706–90), were published in many versions throughout nineteenth-century France.

factory-owners and seeing his wife and children become factory hands.

Long before the left became concerned with alienation and anomie in modern industrial urban society, these conceptions were basic to conservative thought. Bonald especially decried the gradual disappearance of the rural village, self-sufficient in production and consumption, and with much of its property held in common. The decline of the self-contained village, he held, would end generations of closely knit personal contacts. From the interrelations of such traditional groups as the village elders, guilds and Church, Bonald believed, had grown the norms of ethical behaviour, norms that could hardly be maintained in the harsh anonymity of casual and fleeting urban relationships.

The modern farmer no longer produced for acquaintances of long standing, but for faceless multitudes in distant markets. Only profit could be his motive. Economic growth piled men into vast cities, tore them from their ancient local roots and created a culture of strangers. Defenceless and vulnerable, because bereft of the support of their communal groups, what could men become except either the victims or the aggressors in a struggle for material gain which, even when won, rarely did more than increase dissatisfaction and insecurity? Reading Bonald's fears in our own post-industrial era, we may find in them grounds for nostalgia, but not a basis for action. The stable and self-sufficient village culture which he proclaimed has vanished from the West. Yet in the years before the great onslaught of industrialism, the men who led the Restoration in France saw a world still relatively undisturbed by what seemed to them two brief decades of revolutionary aberration, a world which they could still hope to preserve.

The ultras were encouraged by the strong revival of royalist and conservative sentiment which greeted the return of Louis XVIII. This was as much a result of the desire for peace as anything else, a fact recognized by the allies when they cautioned moderation. But the returning ultras were more royalist than the King, as their slogan 'Long live the king in spite of himself!' indicates. A 'white terror' arose spontaneously as royalist gangs, often led by nobles, murdered thousands (the number is not precisely known) of former Jacobins, Bonapartists, Protestants and Jews. The history of the radical right had begun. For a brief period such groups controlled large sections of the more backward areas of France. But the government was unwilling to risk a violent confrontation with former Jacobin sympathizers by giving rein to the inclinations of many on the right. Nevertheless, numerous rightist murderers were acquitted, some former revolutionaries and Bonapartists were executed, thousands were jailed and over one-third of all government officials were purged.

The liberal gains of the revolutionary years were embodied in the Charter of 1814, which limited the powers of the monarch. The property settlements of the Revolution were confirmed, some civil liberties were granted and there was to be an elected Chamber of

Deputies, whose ministers were to be responsible to the king, not to the elected representatives of the people. This troubled the ultras in spite of their contempt for representative government, because the elections of 1816 had given them a total of 350 deputies out of 392. Indeed, until the revolution of 1830, the ultras controlled the Chamber for ten out of fifteen years.

However, elections during the Restoration did not reflect public opinion. Only some 90,000 citizens out of 32 million had enough property to vote, while only a third of these bothered to do so. There was no secret ballot; one-third of the deputies were government officials; and police, government and clergy could intimidate voters with ease. Deputies tended to be nobles, wealthy non-noble landowners of local prominence and higher government officials. The real bulwarks of conservative power were extra-parliamentary, for local notables dominated the upper administration, local offices and the Church – some 71 of the 89 bishops appointed during the Restoration were noblemen. In spite of the Revolution, it has been estimated that until 1848 the establishment of France was composed of some 700 persons, three-quarters of whom were lords and nobles, and the rest wealthy landlords and clerics.

Among lower-class supporters of traditionalist values were to be found former guild masters, small shopkeepers, the peasant population of the more backward rural areas and the personal servants of the well-off. The latter formed a large proportion of the population of pre-industrial France, and included one out of every fifteen of the inhabitants of Paris. Servants, then as now, tended to identify with their masters.

The legislation of the Restoration favoured conservatives, but compromises with the more liberal consensus had to be made. Only those confiscated lands which had not been sold were returned to the aristocracy; however, the wealth of the latter enabled them to buy back half of their former lands. Feudal dues remained a lost cause. The army which had brought Napoleon's reforms to all Europe was purged of its liberal officers, and the future Charles X – the most ultra of all the returning exiles – used his position as head of the National Guard to make it a tool of ultra-royalism should the chance for a *coup d'état* to destroy the Charter arise. Conscription was shunned, for the people armed was a dread spectre from the Jacobin past. In 1823 the French government demonstrated its fealty to the principles of the

Holy Alliance by crushing a liberal revolution in Spain, though the brutal terror of King Ferdinand and his nobles was too much for even royalist French generals to stomach.

The true faith was restored. De Maistre's prediction proved correct; bishops and priests abandoned the worldliness of their pre-revolutionary forbears. A host of ultra-conservative lay religious groups emerged. One of these, the Knights of the Faith, enjoyed political influence in the highest circles of the government. Church attendance rose dramatically, and great numbers of ordinary citizens attended revivalist meetings in public squares where Mass was held to purge the sins of Jacobinism, denounce the Charter and swear allegiance to King and Pope. The government gave large subsidies to train new priests; this generation of seminarists proved to be the most intensely religious and the most fervently antagonistic to modern thought in living memory. Those Church lands not already sold were now protected by ultra legislation, and the education of the young was returned to the clergy. Paradoxically, Napoleon's compromises with the Vatican had subjected French bishops to more direct control from the Pope. This ensured that the French Church, unlike the monarchy, would make no compromises with liberalism.

CHARLES X

Louis XVIII and his ministers had been an obstacle to the ultras' desire to return to the principles of 1788, because the throne rested uneasy in the knowledge that foreign troops had twice had to defeat Frenchmen under Napoleon to restore the Bourbons. But the death of Louis XVIII in 1824 brought to the throne the most impatient and reactionary of the ultras, Charles X. In the same year elections crushed the liberal forces in the Chamber. Before 1789, the Bourbon who was to become Charles X had been a gambling, womanizing, debt-ridden, reactionary prince of the blood – a simple-minded ultra-rightist who detested both bourgeois and Jew. In 1789 he had opposed all compromises, and tried to lead a counter-revolution to put the leaders of the Third Estate to the sword. He fled immediately after the fall of the Bastille, and, as the King's brother, became the leader of the counter-revolution in exile. He joined the invading forces of Austria and Prussia in 1792 with a small army of exiles, but instead of the welcoming rising of a loyal populace which he had expected in his ignorance of true public sentiment, his force met starvation and merciless peasant ambushes. Until the Restoration and with funds from various European powers, the future Charles X spent his time planning and executing minor plots and conspiracies. He dared not risk personally joining the counter-revolutionary peasantry of the 1790s, although they much desired his presence. While his brother reigned as Louis XVIII, he championed the most extreme reaction and hoped for the day when he might rule in the spirit of de Maistre and Bonald.

Once in office Charles X rewarded his most ardent supporters from the exile, some 7,000 nobles and clerics, with an indemnity of one billion francs for lands confiscated by the revolutionaries. Some 300 deputies stood to profit thereby, so the bill with Bonald's aid easily passed the Chamber. The King's former companions were rewarded in other ways with state funds, and some attempts were made to maintain intact the indebted estates of ancient noble families. The Church was the King's primary concern; as the result of an intense religious experience in 1804 he had forsworn his early dissolute ways. The Jesuits were brought back to France, and Catholic leaders were given a powerful voice in royal political appointments. Considerable public outrage was aroused when a bill was passed which provided that anyone who profaned sacred vessels or consecrated wafers should have hand and then head sliced off by the guillotine – the traditional method of executing parricides. Bonald thought it merciful that such a criminal should be sent immediately to God the Father for judgment. When the heir to the throne was given over to religious tutors of ultra and extreme reactionary persuasion, even moderate royalists as well as liberals feared for the future. The press, harassed by censorship and financial penalties, could give no accurate representation of even conservative misgivings. Bonald insisted that there was no reason for the press to concern itself with politics; did not the King have the wisdom of 80,000 landowners at his disposal? After all, Bonald remarked, was not censorship merely a precaution taken to protect society from false doctrines, very like the sanitary measures one took to guard against the plague?

In spite of an electoral system which favoured great landowners and nobles, and even though the government had the means to exert heavy pressure on the bulk of the 80,000 voters of France, the first election of the reign of Charles X (1827) proved a disaster for the ultras. The King would not back down. The issue was joined when he disregarded the election results and appointed reactionary ministers. Even moderate royalists would not support him in this, let alone the new Chamber. The Charter offered no solution; either King or Chamber must give way. Charles X believed that he was a monarch by divine right. He had been forced to live with the Charter, but he was quite prepared to undertake a *coup* to establish royal supremacy.

The King's contempt for parliamentary ways was clearly shown when he selected as his leading minister Prince Jules de Polignac, an old companion in exile. A former favourite of Marie-Antoinette, an avid reader of de Maistre and Bonald, and a man who believed that the Virgin Mary had appeared to him in person to give political advice, Polignac, like his fellow ministers, was not one to think that the will of some 80,000 voters should outweigh the power of a monarch selected by the Almighty. But expediency dictated a final attempt to govern within the terms of the Charter. The Chamber was dissolved. New elections were to be held in the summer of 1830. Royalists declared it a crime to return men who had voted against the King; clerics called it heresy; and the King himself appealed for votes as the anointed 'father' of France. Meanwhile, the invasion of Algeria was announced, because, as future governments were to discover, it was often possible to gain popular support through imperialist adventures. In July, however, just when the fall of Algiers to the French was reported, the extreme right was defeated in the elections. More than one military officer sensed a need to bring the troops back to Paris.

The Charter stated that should the safety of the state be endangered, the king might govern by royal ordinance. Charles X was too isolated to realize that he had almost no significant support outside his entourage of reactionaries. In 1830 he announced his famous July Ordinances: freedom of the press was suspended; the Chamber of Deputies was dissolved; and a new electoral system was declared, one that would shift even more electoral power to noble and landed proprietors and away from the professional, commercial and industrial middle classes. The revolution started in Paris within a day. The revolutionaries were craftsmen, small shopowners, employees of large firms (often given the day off by their liberal employers) and the unemployed. Two hundred soldiers and 2,000 citizens died in the fighting; increasingly, Charles X found that he could not depend on the loyalty of his troops. Offended by the King's stubborn arrogance, yet fearing that a radical republic might result if the fighting in Paris continued, leading deputies, financiers, professional men and industrialists rallied round a man very much like themselves, but of royal blood, the Duke of Orleans, and asked him to assume the throne. Lacking any significant support and too inflexible to compromise, Charles X abdicated in favour of his son. It was too late. As Louis-Philippe, the Duke became the 'citizen king of the French'. The Charter was altered so that it was no longer a gift of the throne; Catholicism was declared no longer the state religion of France, but simply the religion of the majority of Frenchmen. Constitutional monarchy had finally been established in France. De Maistre and Bonald became subjects for intellectual history. Charles X fled the country. The ultras retreated to their castles to brood.

12 'You're not there yet.' Charles X and a Jesuit attempt the climb to absolute power. Anonymous French colour print, 1830.

V THE REVOLUTIONS OF 1848

The revolutions of 1848 were the last in Europe, excluding those caused by defeat in war. Their suppression also marked the last triumph of the semi-feudal varieties of conservatism discussed previously. It is misleading to label these revolutions liberal, as is usually done. The revolutions were started and maintained by artisans and peasants who were either fighting to maintain some elements of the traditional order, or whose status had been dislocated by the intrusion of liberal commercial capitalism. It is true that liberals assumed leadership once the outbreaks had started, but they wanted reform, not revolution. Moreover, the liberals did not represent the middle class as a whole, but only the politically aware professional groups – lawyers, civil servants, educators and students. There was no mass following for liberal reforms in Europe, and the middle classes in general had no clearly perceived class enemy blocking their social mobility as in 1789. Consequently they were much more wary of the potential for social upheaval from below.

The liberal leaders of the revolutions were isolated from their own class and, as it turned out, had little to offer the artisans and peasants in revolt that could not as easily have been granted by conservatives. Only in Hungary and Italy, where nationalism incited mass risings against the Austrians, were the revolutions truly violent and sweeping. Elsewhere, we find only urban revolts accompanied by sporadic peasant uprisings. Excluding France, frightened conservative élites were never overthrown; they merely made paper concessions and withdrew temporarily until the weakness of the revolutionaries was evident, whereupon they returned in force. East of France traditionalists could still dominate the forms of social upheaval characteristic of pre-industrial society. In 1848 the industrial proletariat played almost no role whatsoever, and the outbreaks had familiar traditional causes: 1846 and 1847 were the years of the most terrible crop failures of nineteenth-century Europe, from which stemmed famine, inflation, shrinking markets and unemployment.

In Paris a series of banquets held by leading liberals to protest against restricted suffrage and government corruption brought police repression and a counter-attack from hungry and unemployed artisans, clerks and students. Louis-Philippe fled with hardly a fight, for he had no significant support. His government had been utterly corrupt, supported only by a narrow group of wealthy non–nobles and bureaucratic favourites, while naturally enough neither the ultras nor the clergy showed any enthusiasm for this upstart citizen king. After the King's flight, Lamartine and a group of democratic liberals declared a provisional government, promised universal suffrage and offered public relief projects to calm the unruly.

Elsewhere in the spring of 1848, what were essentially food riots caused the King of Prussia and a host of German princes to appoint liberal ministers and flee their capital cities. Significantly, they retained their thrones and armies. Liberal leaders, who had not contributed to the original violence, moved swiftly to restore social order, protect property and draw up legislation providing for liberal constitutional monarchies. Meanwhile in Frankfurt, a self-appointed assembly of liberal professional groups gathered to prepare elections for an all-German parliament which they hoped would both unite and liberalize Germany.

In Vienna student and artisan riots caused a frightened court to dismiss Metternich (who had argued for the immediate use of counter-force) and promulgate liberal legislation. In a brilliant stroke, the Habsburg government immediately converted the one really dangerous class, the peasantry, into contented subjects. The government abolished the hated forced labour and other manorial obligations which had drained off nearly one-half of peasant income and labour. Landlords were fairly content. They had feared peasant violence and were to be indemnified by tax revenues which would be raised in large measure from the peasants themselves. As violence escalated in Vienna, the court fled to Innsbruck where it was surrounded by its most Catholic and loyal subjects, the Tyrolese small farmers, who had fought even Napoleon's troops to a standstill. Replacing the Emperor Ferdinand, who had been forced to sign liberal legislation, by Franz Josef, the court of aristocrats, generals and clergy prepared the counter-revolution.

However, the Empire needed attention before the revolt in Vienna could be put down. In Prague risings were swiftly crushed, for Bohemian nationalism had not yet penetrated mass consciousness. But in Italy fierce fighting drove the Austrians from Milan, while

Charles Albert, King of Piedmont, prepared to march against the Austrians in the hope of increasing his territories and preventing urban radicals from dominating the revolution. In Rome Pope Pius IX fled after denouncing as sacrilegious the elections carried out by the successful rebels. A Roman Republic was declared; Garibaldi and Mazzini arrived in the Holy City; Church property was distributed to the poor; and the Inquisition was ended.

In Hungary a liberal government under Louis Kossuth declared itself independent of Vienna and emancipated the serfs, thus raising powerful peasant armies. They were the only revolutionaries able to do so. The gentry supported this action because they were to be compensated for their losses, and they hoped to establish a Magyar empire at the expense of Slavs and Romanians who, along with the Jews, were excluded from voting privileges by the new constitution. Kossuth's revolution, in short, was powerful not because it was liberal, but because it favoured the lesser aristocracy and was nationalist, racist and imperialist. Significantly, it was the only revolution which caused traditionalists grave difficulties.

Where nationalism was not popular, and liberals guided revolutions according to their own principles, the artisans, unemployed and peasants who caused the upheavals soon turned apathetic or even hostile. In France a tax levied to pay for workers' relief created great antagonism among the peasantry, encouraged by nobles and priests. The small farmers simply assumed that the unemployed of Paris were idle and violent 'reds'. Elsewhere in Europe the commercial capitalism so prized by liberals often subjected peasants and artisans to the control of outside buyers with access to distant markets. Rural crafts which had traditionally been a source of extra peasant income now suffered from the competition of urban manufacturing. As for feudal dues, liberals were too respectful of property rights to end them outright; we have seen how conservatives were willing to abolish them if properly frightened and compensated. It would take far more radical ideologies to mobilize peasant discontent against landlords into sweeping revolutions.

Liberals had no chance of maintaining the support of the most active revolutionaries, the urban artisans. Outside of France the guilds were still strong, and even including French artisans composed over one-half of the labour force as late as 1870. Conservative intellectuals and politicians had favoured the guilds and feared liberal free

13   Contemporary engraving of Louis Kossuth (1802–94). Committed to the ideal of a Magyar national state at the expense of imperial and Slav interests, Kossuth became a popular hero throughout Europe.

enterprise and capitalist machine technology ever since the Luddite disturbances of early nineteenth-century England. The guild masters could see little point in supporting those who threatened to turn them into dependent and semi-skilled 'wage slaves' and deprive them of their status as skilled shopowners.

In the turbulent spring of 1848, therefore, those artisans who had done the most to bring about revolution – weavers, construction workers, metal workers, masons and others – demonstrated for a restoration of their former rights to regulate markets, prices, wages, product quality and entry into the guilds. They insisted as well on heavy restrictions against what they saw as the ruthless exploitation and destructive competition of free enterprise. Ideological weapons were readily available to them. French royalists had often held that there must be a complete restoration of the guild system, as it was the only truly Christian political economy. Early in the nineteenth century, one Eugène Buret, among others, had conceived a truly Utopian vision of a France in which each citizen would be enrolled in the guild appropriate to his trade, vocation, business or profession. In cooperation with a Supreme Council of National Production, these guilds would plan and control the products of labour and their distribution.

Even the famous Proudhon, too easily assumed to be a man of the left, lamented the death of the guilds and the loss of the moral bond between master, journeyman and apprentice. He hoped for a return to self-regulating communities of skilled craftsmen. Indeed, much of what has been called Utopian socialism ought to be seen as essentially conservative in outlook. The writings of Charles Fourier, for example, really constitute an idealized and restructured vision of the agrarian communalism of the past; a vision which, along with others like it, had a strong appeal to that first generation of workers who had been abruptly removed from their traditional rural order and flung into the harsh, grey life of the early factory towns.

The most politically significant attempt to restore the guild order in the spring of 1848 occurred in the Germanies. Congresses of artisans met to issue manifestos and proposals. The most important met in Frankfurt itself. One of the delegates was Karl Marlo, a man hardly known today but then the favourite ideologist and propagandist of the assembled masters and journeymen. Like the left-wing socialists whose views were expressed in the *Communist Manifesto*, Marlo and the guildsmen held an apocalyptic vision of the 'empire of misery' which liberal capitalism would create for the workers. Skill, industry and human relationships would crumble before the possessors of capital and machine technology. The worker, no longer the owner of his own means of production, would be the helpless victim of the 'freedom' granted the bourgeois, a freedom to destroy the stable and regulated economic system of the old order.

As a result, Marlo insisted, economic life would be reduced to an anarchic struggle for survival between capitalists able to concentrate wealth and the means of production into their own hands. Yet, he continued, their system would destroy itself, because, though eventually producing for a world market, they could neither predict its needs nor limit the production of their competitors. Surplus production would overreach effective demand. The worker would be unable to purchase the products for which he had laboured, and profits would go only to those capitalists who reduced the wages of their semi-skilled workers to the bone. Unlike the artisan who always knew the limits of his prospects, because he functioned within the familiar boundaries and regulations of local needs and controlled output and prices, the proletarian, unable to predict his economic future, would produce children without careful forethought. The result of all this, Marlo and the assembled guildsmen believed, would be the destruction of the family, the misery of the worker and the collapse of society. Throughout the great cities of Europe, roving bands of unemployed and starving men without hope would deliver society over to constant upheavals and futile violence.

Today it is difficult to sympathize with the terror Marlo felt when he observed what he took to be the effects of the Industrial Revolution. However, once his fears become real to us we are able to understand why he thought that only the most radical return to the principles of the medieval guild system would be of any permanent value. He visualized the coming of the men of the new disorder; armed with the might of capital, machinery and steam, contemptuous of the petty restrictions of the guild system, they would easily destroy their weak competitors in the guilds and with them the peace of the old order, until nothing remained but exploitation, arrogance and luxury, pitted against helplessness, hate and misery. Were not France and England, Marlo asked his readers, proof enough of the sheer anarchy of unfettered industrialization? There one found the rule of a powerful and parasitic oligarchy of wealth, luxuriating in profits gained by the toil of an enslaved proletariat who earned just enough to return to the machines, day after miserable day.

> The stability of all social relationships is destroyed; the organic union of the industrial classes is decomposed; and society is divided into two masses of enemies that find their centre of gravity in the bourgeoisie and proletariat. An endless battle for external goods has endangered the inner values of the combatants; avarice on the one side and bitterness on the other have hardened [all] souls against the commands of moral law and even threatened the maintenance of legal order. All these evils are increasing, for the only remaining law of this endless movement declares: The rich shall become richer and the poor poorer . . . Moral rottenness, that is the great and horrible result of a false social order, that is the curse of liberalism.

Like Marx, Marlo tended to project the worst aspects of the

'hungry forties' into a necessary result of the inevitable contradictions of the capitalist system itself.

What should be done to avoid all this? Marlo proposed that industry, trade and agriculture be organized into national guilds. Each guild and each enterprise within a guild must have a legal limit imposed upon its size and activities beyond which it would not be allowed to expand. Industrial and agricultural enterprises would be limited to a certain number of workers, and each merchandizing firm would be given a monopoly over a part of the national market. In this way the terror of unlimited expansion might be avoided. Those who amassed more capital than was necessary for their enterprises would be required to lend it to those who lacked the money but not the ability to exploit their share of the market. The state must keep interest rates low, and must also ensure for each citizen a 'sphere of activity' equivalent to his abilities. Organized along these lines, the state would be able to ward off the destructive competition for markets and capital, and the dangerous concentration of wealth and power in the hands of a few which had transformed modern societies into a chaotic struggle for survival. Finally, to offset the terrors of what the young Marx called the 'immiseration' of the proletariat, Marlo proposed a series of measures to keep the size of the population in harmony with the means of subsistence. He also insisted that each citizen and enterprise must contribute to health, old age and life insurance programmes. Those who could not find private employment would be provided public work by the state.

In short, Marlo had described what later conservatives were to call the corporate state. For, like most revolutionaries of 1848, Marlo was not convinced of the value of 'mere' political changes; nevertheless, he did provide for a democratically elected Chamber of Deputies, headed by a president or Kaiser. The real work of government, however, would be performed by an industrial or social chamber, to be elected by the guilds voting according to profession, and with the stipulation that three-fifths of its members would be selected from the industrial guilds. Theirs would be the task of planning the new organization of work and presenting it for approval to the political chamber. The political chamber would then order the plan to be put into effect by the minister of labour with his corps of experts, and, it is to be feared, a considerable body of men, armed to the teeth. Marlo was unaware of the powerful opposition his plan would arouse, nor did the technical difficulties dim his enthusiasm. The federalists, as he called his supporters,

> . . . were not concerning themselves with humanitarian dreams . . . they do not aim at founding a paradise, but a society in which only the natural world order will set the boundaries to the most free unfolding of all personalities. They are convinced that with the introduction of the federal order everyone will have a task measured to his abilities and a profit equal to his performance; involuntary poverty will end; a general well-being will replace luxury and poverty; dishonest profit through usury, stock-jobbing, and cheating will be ended in favour of honest gain; productive work will replace unproductive idleness; stable progress will be brought to all industry; national income will increase rapidly; all products will find the most adequate markets open to them; all capital will be offered the best investment opportunities . . . crimes will be reduced to an inconsiderable number; the military forces now needed to uphold an unjust social order will be unnecessary; the national debt will be reduced by more than half, the basis of a true, not just a formal, sovereignty of the people will be laid; the greatest guarantees for a lasting peace will be assured; and all that organization of civil society can do to create conditions for a moral society will have been done.

This is Utopian conservatism with a vengeance.

Observe the work of the liberals and capitalists of England, Marlo and the guildsmen implored, and do not let the same thing happen here.

> They [the liberals] wanted to make work free, and have bowed it under the yoke of capital; they wanted to unchain all powers, and have beaten men down with the chains of misery; they wanted to free the serf from bondage, and have robbed him of the very ground on which he stood; they wanted the well-being of all, and have created only the extremes of poverty and luxury . . . they wanted to destroy all monopolies, and have replaced them with the monster monopoly of capital . . . they wanted education to be the property of all, and have made it the privilege of wealth; they wanted the highest moral improvement of society, and have plunged it in moral rottenness; in short, they wanted limitless freedom, and have created the most abusive thraldom . . .

Inspired by Marlo, the assembled masters forwarded his proposal for a General Guild and Industrial Order to the liberals of the Frankfurt Parliament. Other proposals were sent later by an assembly of journeymen who feared the autocratic tendencies of the masters and persuaded Marlo to help them formulate more democratic principles for a revived guild system – all to no avail. The appropriate committee of the Frankfurt Parliament was amazed to discover a political economist who rejected classical liberalism, and denounced all such proposals as selfish, reactionary and in violation of the known laws of economic progress. After all, as one member correctly noted, Napoleon had introduced free enterprise into Bavaria some forty years earlier, and the bulk of the artisans there were still thriving, for much of their work was not replaceable by machine technology. When the Frankfurt Parliament published its final proposals in the famous *Fundamental Rights of the German People*, it demanded free enterprise, rejected government controls over business, denied the guilds any coercive powers and insisted that all be allowed free entry into the crafts and trades.

In any event, the guildsmen's demonic vision of the effects of industrial capitalism was never realized. Some trades – especially luxury ones – could not be replaced by mass production and specialized machinery. Many artisans became sub-contractors or highly paid skilled workers for large firms, and the real wages of the industrial proletariat rose dramatically in the coming half-century. Nevertheless, 'blue-collar' artisans and small shopkeepers remained major supporters of the conservative parties throughout the nineteenth century, especially when more sophisticated machinery and large retail outlets increased pressures on their small enterprises.

THE CONSERVATIVES VICTORIOUS

French liberals and radicals quickly discovered their lack of support. Conservatives soundly defeated them in the elections of April 1848, the first held under universal manhood suffrage. Peasants tended to vote for familiar local notables; priests and nobles effectively campaigned in the provinces against the 'red' menace of Jacobin Paris. The new government cut public relief funds for the unemployed and, using the new railway network to bring rural and conservative troops to fight against radical Paris, bloodily crushed the revolt in June of some 15,000 workers. Some 3,000 were shot without trial; thousands more were sent to Algerian labour camps. In May 1849 elections were held for a president of the Republic and an assembly. Napoleon III, the candidate of social order, won over his liberal opponents by more than five to one; two-thirds of the seats in the assembly were won by a variety of conservatives, most of whom hoped for a swift return to monarchy. Napoleon III and the assembly proceeded to purge the government and army of republicans, to give back to the Church powerful controls over education and to disenfranchise some 3 million of those most likely to vote for the left.

The new constitution forbade the president to run for a second term. With the help of the army, Napoleon III seized power in 1851. Some 100,000 took up arms against him but they were brutally and swiftly suppressed. The French public was allowed to vote to approve the *coup*, which was presented as the only alternative to 'red ruin'. Ninety per cent of those who voted approved, although many republicans abstained. Partly because he had used French troops to restore the temporal power of the Pope in 1849, a grateful Church placed its vast communications network at Napoleon's disposal. As one cleric put it: 'Jesus says vote yes.' To conservatives in general it seemed that this Napoleon would stamp out parliamentary rule for good. In 1852 Napoleon III declared himself emperor with full powers over legislation and foreign affairs, and with the right to name his successors. Paris was redesigned so that broad avenues gave ready access to artillery and cavalry should revolution threaten again. Without the aid of foreign invasion, as in 1870, the people of Paris would no longer be able to drive the government to the left of the general consensus in France.

In spite of all this, Napoleon III was not merely another traditionalist of the Metternich type. He was the first of a dynamic new type of conservative, men who did not merely condemn and suppress modern forces, but knew how to manipulate them for their own ends. Helped by his famous name, Napoleon III skilfully managed the new mass electorate by appropriate references to the 'red' menace, and by active campaigning with vague promises offered to each major group. At the same time he was careful to emphasize his special concern for the interests of propertied notables, frustrated monarchists and the Church. He achieved popular support by encouraging nationalism and imperialism. He joined the British in

China, and with Catholic support moved to subvert the Buddhism and independence of Indochina. Above all, and unlike previous conservatives, Napoleon III understood that rapid economic growth would reduce the potential for revolution. Through law and subsidy, he aided those entrepreneurs and projects most likely to industrialize France.

In the Germanies, the Frankfurt Parliament soon discovered that there was no overwhelming support for either a united or a liberal Germany. Indeed, the bulk of the parliamentarians betrayed their own liberalism by cheering the Austrian defeats of the Czechs, Italians and Hungarians. In an absurd gesture, the Parliament offered an imperial German crown to the King of Prussia. He rejected it with contempt. Now that the former insurgents were either apathetic or hostile, the Frankfurt Parliament became fatally dependent on the force of the ultra-conservative Prussian army. In Prussia itself, liberals dominated the first popularly elected assembly of 1848. Their support eroded as the rebels lost ground. The troops of the King met little resistance when they reclaimed Berlin and were later used to quell outbursts elsewhere in the Germanies.

14   Woodcut from the enormously popular series *A Dance of Death in the Year 1848*, illustrated by Alfred Rethel (1816–59). The year of revolutions ended with the suppression of democratic movements in Italy, France, Austria and Prussia.

15 Contemporary caricature of Frederick William IV of Prussia refusing to allow a paper constitution to be forced between himself and his subjects.

An avid admirer of Novalis and Sir Walter Scott, Frederick William IV of Prussia had once insisted that he would allow no written constitution to come between him and his good subjects. His advisers indicated that this might be dangerous, so a constitution was granted in 1850 by royal decree. It left little to chance. The king retained absolute power over the army and an absolute veto over all legislation. Further protection against 'red revolution' was provided by a three-class system of voting which gave a wealthy landowner or businessman a vote equal to that of 35 poor Berliners. Conservative majorities were returned throughout the 1850s, while court and aristocracy shored up their rule by giving state aid and self-regulatory powers to thousands of guilds, re-establishing aristocratic manorial rights and founding the most influential journal of the reaction, the *Kreuzzeitung*.

As we have seen, the Austrian Empire was the most threatened in 1848, because nationalism united conservatives and non-conservatives in the Italian and Hungarian wars of liberation. After difficult and bloody battles, however, the Italians were subdued. But the Hungarian armies were not defeated until Tsar Nicholas, true to the principles of the Holy Alliance and fearing what the example might do to his own multi-national empire, sent 360,000 Russian troops to rescue the beleaguered Austrians. The Austrian repression was extreme; no concessions were to be made to those mortal enemies of the Empire, liberalism and nationalism. Deeply pious and hostile to all modern ideas, Franz Josef gave Germans a near monopoly of imperial bureaucratic posts, made German the official language, cancelled all previous liberal concessions and gave more powers to the Church than it had enjoyed since the Counter-Reformation. Austria, however, was to win no more wars. She remained a living fossil of pre-revolutionary days only because other great powers feared the consequences of her destruction.

Even in Italy, French troops were needed to restore the Pope in 1849. Pius IX immediately brought the most reactionary policies to bear, as was his only choice. The claim of the Church to be the sole repository of ancient, sacred and absolute truths irrevocably tied it to the institutions and values of pre-Enlightenment Europe. Liberal Catholicism was a contradiction in terms, and Pius IX denounced it as heresy, a position readily acceptable to the two major groups supporting the Vatican: the peasant masses and Latin aristocratic élites.

Not surprisingly, the Pope responded to the revolutions by firmly establishing ultra-conservative authoritarianism within the Church. From his pontificate dates the veneration of the Pope: 'When the Pope meditates, God thinks in him.' Science and secular rules of evidence were ignored when in 1854 Pius IX declared the immaculate conception of the Virgin Mary and when, ten years later, he initiated his counter-revolution of the spirit with the famous encyclical, the *Syllabus of Errors*. Modern ideas and liberal values were then condemned out of hand, without any attempt to argue or persuade. Absolute truth need only be proclaimed. Thus it was declared that there was no salvation outside the Church. The Pope could make no errors in matters of faith and morals; he was the final authority in disputes with political leaders; his word was sovereign over all national Churches. The Papal States were the 'robe of Christ', and the judicial powers of the papacy, as well as its authority over marriage, divorce and censorship, came from Christ himself. In other matters, the Pope added, Christians owed obedience to their legitimate princes.

16 Pro-Austrian support and Jesuit treachery hinder the liberation of Italy. Caricature from *Don Pirlone*, 1849.

A few years later, in 1870, the Vatican Council declared the dogma of papal infallibility. Evidently God did not notice, for after the defeat of France by the armies of Prussia, the Italians took Rome and completed the work that had begun when the bulk of the Papal States had been seized in 1860. The King of Italy promptly declared an end to the temporal powers of the Pope. Throughout the following decade, the self-styled 'prisoner of the Vatican' refused the large indemnities and sovereignty over Vatican City offered as compensation by the Kingdom of Italy. Not until the rise of socialism in the early twentieth century were the faithful permitted to vote in Italian elections. Only after Mussolini had smashed Italian liberalism would the Vatican have official dealings with the state. The end of the Second World War marked the first period in which liberal Catholic movements were tolerated by the Vatican for any length of time.

17–20 The growth of national stereotypes. Above, the Frenchman as incurable Bonapartist and the Russians as a semi-civilized warrior people. Below, a party of over-bearing English travellers and the German as philosopher and patriot. From a series of lithographs depicting various nations, *Düsseldorfer Künstleralbum*, 1852.

VI THE NEW CONSERVATISM
1850–90

In the latter half of the nineteenth century new social conditions forced conservatives to break with many of the policies of the ultras and Metternich. Adjustments and concessions had to be made. Industrialism and urbanism transformed rural Europe. Nationalism became an intense and popular emotion among ever larger groups of the population. Increasingly, liberals dominated representative institutions, while a sizeable and organized industrial proletariat gave power to trade unionism and socialism. Liberals assumed too readily, however, that all this meant the inevitable and imminent demise of conservatism. Most European nations were still monarchies, strongly influenced by aristocrats and a co-opted and moderately conservative upper middle class of great economic power. Liberals did increase their power in parliaments, but they often found themselves bypassed by institutions still nearly the exclusive territory of the right: government administration, the army, the Church, the diplomatic corps and the judiciary.

As the power of representative institutions increased and universal suffrage loomed on the horizon, conservatives needed to form alliances with new groups and win lower-class support. Reluctantly, conservative landowners joined forces with the leaders of heavy industry by supporting increased arms budgets (the arms race began in the 1870s). Conservatives also encouraged imperialism abroad and the economic exploitation of natural resources. Imperial bureaucratic posts and military establishments were often sinecures for the titled sons of conservative families. Big landowners and industrialists cooperated in negotiating mutually beneficial tariff arrangements, usually at the expense of the consumer.

As we have seen, traditionalists had feared nationalism because it destroyed unique local arrangements and weakened the power of local notables. Nationalism was also associated with Jacobin radicalism, the reforms of the first Napoleon, and the liberal revolutionaries of the Romantic era. Nevertheless, local ties and loyalties were gradually broken down by the impact of industrialism, urbanism and the widening networks of transport and communications. Moreover, near the end of the century, conservatives were able to find ways of associating ultra-patriotism with conservative institutions and values. Because potential and powerful enemies were always at the frontier, conservative party leaders often found the cry of 'The Fatherland in danger!' useful to suppress social discontent and brand the internationalist and anti-militarist left as the party of treason. The introduction of universal military conscription gave aristocratic military leaders the chance to condition civilian recruits in the authoritarian obedience necessary for battle. The structure of military life was psychologically useful, for it discouraged liberal and democratic tendencies among the young. Compulsory elementary education, moreover, had created a higher illiteracy which made the lower classes vulnerable to the predominantly conservative-owned mass press. To gain circulation among the masses, the daily press treated them to accounts of the blood sport of imperialist heroics, a sport sanctified by high-minded editorializing about the survival of the fittest and the civilizing mission of the West.

Conservatives could often gain votes from farmers and peasant smallholders by leading the battle against liberal commercial groups who favoured international free trade and the duty-free import of agricultural products. In France small landowners supported the Third Republic, but only so long as it did little to relieve the distress of the urban workers, especially through higher taxes. Now that feudal dues had become only a memory, peasants elsewhere in Europe supported conservative parties for a variety of reasons. In times of depression, when liberal bankers and money-lenders foreclosed mortgages and recalled debts, peasants were often driven from their ancestral villages into the alien environment of the city. There they were exposed to bewildering challenges to their traditional attitudes, challenges which, like upper-class conservatives, they could only interpret as the expression of moral decay: shattered kinship groups, liberated women, secular attitudes, rootless 'red' workers and left-wing politicians. Newly emigrated peasants tended to join conservative and ultra-patriotic parties and organizations which idealized rural life and the old ways, kept those ways alive in rhetoric, ritual and symbol, and denounced liberals, Jews and socialists.

Conservatives were especially favoured by the rapid growth of lower middle-class groups who moved swiftly to the right when their property or status were threatened: white-collar workers, small businessmen, shop personnel and the multitudes of civil servants and office clerks who filled the swiftly expanding governmental and corporate bureaucracies. Such groups increased more than the industrial proletariat in relative percentages of the population in advanced nations during the latter decades of the century. The lower middle classes moved to the right because they feared the proletariat, identified their status with the upper-class property owners and management, imitated upper-class 'respectability' and manifested their expected social mobility by a strong faith in established institutions.

Consequently, new and powerful sources of support were available to those conservatives willing to discard the outright reaction and fear of any compromise with modernism characteristic of the old conservatives of the era of Metternich and the ultras. Moreover, conservatives willing to adopt dynamic policies were not doomed to see political and military power shift to nations dominated by liberalism and the middle classes. For the two basic sources of power in Western civilization, national unity and industrial expansion, could be mastered and manipulated in ways that would ultimately favour the rule of pre-liberal and pre-industrial élites. The first statesman to demonstrate this was the most dynamic new conservative of them all, Prince Otto von Bismarck.

BISMARCK

The policies of Bismarck reversed the trend towards liberalism in central Europe. Using the military might of Prussia, he was able to accomplish the greatest political achievement of modern German history: national unification. He did this in ways which gave all the prestige of the achievement to the conservative élites of Prussia, thus solidifying their hold over a nation which, by the start of the twentieth century, was the most industrialized in all Europe. Germany was to be the first powerful industrial state dominated by institutions and values which stemmed from the pre-liberal and pre-industrial past. This in itself revived what had been the declining power of European conservatives, for it demonstrated that the forces of nationalism and industrialism need not always favour liberals.

Bismarck's task was not easy. When he was called to power in 1862 by William I of Prussia, the Junker establishment saw no need to change the principles of government which they shared with the leaders of Austria and Russia. Industrial technology had not yet shown that it could dominate the battlefield in war; national enthusiasm had played no role in the defeat of Napoleon. The Prussian revolution of 1848 had been quickly suppressed. Moreover, as efficient bureaucrats, soldiers and estate managers, the Junkers could hardly be dismissed as idle parasites living off the toil of an oppressed peasantry, like the French aristocracy of the eighteenth century. Thus the court and the Junkers remained loyal to the old ideas, ably expressed by the brothers Ernst and Ludwig von Gerlach and constantly reiterated, after 1848, from pulpit, school and conservative press, notably the *Kreuzzeitung*. Princes should govern with the advice and consent of their nobles. Mass electorates were the ignorant tools of demagogues like Napoleon III. Nobles, peasants and artisans composed the solid core of the state. Free enterprise was destructive and even unchristian. Liberals were subversive upstarts. The disloyal urban mob must be controlled by force. Factories might enrich a few capitalists, but they also created a proletarian menace to the state. Bankers, merchants and especially Jews, with their endless search for profit, would destroy the great traditions of Prussia if allowed access to power. In good Prussian fashion, the right argued, the state must carefully regulate the use of land, the introduction of machinery, the rate of interest and the control of credit. Only thus could economic stability and the subordination of the industrial bourgeoisie be assured. Above all, the citizens of Prussia must conform to the military model of hierarchy, duty, obedience and sacrifice for the good of the community.

The unification of the Germanies was feared by Prussian leaders. This had been a goal of the revolutionaries of 1848, and was still supported mainly by the professional, commercial and industrial classes, the only groups potentially capable of wresting political power from the landed and military establishment and forcing eventual reforms on the monarchy. More frightening still, how could Junker interests, Prussian institutions and traditional customs survive in a Germany combining a wide variety of legal and political systems, and including the more liberal areas of the south-west? Finally, as the Gerlach brothers pointed out, because the princes of the Germanies ruled by divine right, it followed that no Christian prince could challenge their authority without destroying his own legitimacy. The

21 The crusaders of the *Kreuzzeitung*. From left to right, Bismarck in the crab-armour of reaction, Ludwig von Gerlach and Friedrich Julius Stahl. The paper was so named from the iron cross on its heading. Caricature from *Kladderadatsch*, Berlin 1865.

King of Italy, they added, had usurped the rights of other Italian dynasties in the name of unification, and was nothing more than a blood-soaked thief supported by a revolutionary mob.

William I, the King of Prussia who, somewhat reluctantly, was to become the Kaiser of Germany under Bismarck's guidance, shared these views. He detested German liberals because they wished to limit his powers and deprive him of absolute control over his army. How could he be expected to hand over the mighty legacy of the Great Elector and Frederick the Great to a collection of lawyers and merchants? William's attitudes were conditioned by the stark simplicities of barrack-room discipline. A simple-minded man, he spoke only with sycophantic court reactionaries and his close friend Adolf Stoecker, the court pastor, otherwise famed as one of the founders of modern German political anti-Semitism. William was not the kind of man to make concessions even to save conservatism.

Indeed, before he came to power in 1862, Bismarck himself was a reactionary of the old style. A Junker squire who had inherited estates which had been in the family for five centuries, Bismarck had opposed any limits to the king's powers and all reforms in 1848; he had even annoyed the court by attempts to launch an immediate counter-revolution. As Frederick William IV had said of him, he was a 'red reactionary, smells of blood, only to be used when bayonets must rule'. After serving in the army and the civil service, Bismarck joined the diplomatic corps where he had occasion to deal with Austria. Convinced of the Empire's weakness, he advised the King to use force to assert Prussian superiority. Bismarck's fellow re-actionaries were appalled. Austria was the embodiment of all their values, and they also feared a break in the central European alliance which had crushed revolutionary liberalism. Bismarck's advice was ignored.

William I appointed Bismarck prime minister of Prussia in September 1862, not to change Prussian foreign policy, but to put a stop to the increasing threat of liberalism in Prussia and the Prussian parliament. German liberalism had not died with the Romantic and revolutionary idealism of 1848, and in 1861 sweeping liberal gains replaced the conservative parliamentary majorities of the 1850s. In 1861, 256 liberals were returned to parliament as against 15 conservatives. Economic modernization had brought more liberal-minded groups into the highest class of the three-class voting system: industrialists, owners of liquid capital, merchants and professionals in the urban trading centres. Such groups began to outweigh the voters of rural and traditional Prussia. Conservatives had only accepted elections in the first place because their King had so commanded, and they had done all they could to return only 'right thinking' dignitaries to office. Squires led their peasants to the polls and watched them carefully (there was no secret ballot); owners of large estates withdrew their trade and custom from merchants or artisans who voted for liberals; and government officials used official funds and licensing powers to reward and punish the appropriate people. But by

1862 it was evident that liberals were not going to be stopped by such measures alone.

The liberal majority in the Prussian parliament wanted a real voice in government decisions; this meant that a constitutional confrontation was inevitable. The Monarch and his supporters had a clear view of how the constitution ought to work. The king should declare his desires to his ministers; they in turn should instruct parliament to carry out the royal will. If a minister disagreed with the king's command, he should resign; if a member of parliament were to question the word of a minister, a duel would be the appropriate response. Discussion was pointless; disobedience, treason. What did parliament represent after all, conservatives argued, but the will of the wealthy bourgeoisie? Did not the king speak for the administration, the army, the judiciary and the peasantry? Were these Prussian voices to be ignored? Some conservatives assumed that the peasant masses would vote for the King's party; some liberals assumed the opposite. But neither side was willing to risk the unknown and fearful consequences of universal suffrage. This meant that the issue would be decided by a conflict between two propertied élites. Unfortunately for the liberals, the King and his nobles controlled the army. In confrontation they would have no need to compromise.

Indeed, it was as a result of a confrontation over parliament's desire to have some influence over the Prussian army that Bismarck was called to office. William and his chief adviser, General von Roon, wanted to increase the size and budget of the army. Parliamentary liberals were willing to approve, but only if compulsory military service was cut from three years to two, and the importance of the civilian reserve militia, the Landwehr, correspondingly increased. Von Roon insisted that three years were needed to imbue civilians with the proper military spirit of unquestioning obedience to established authority. As for the Landwehr, conservatives detested these citizen soldiers. Their officers were middle class in origin and tended to be liberal in outlook, in stark contrast to the regular army. Some Landwehr units had been reluctant to shoot down supporters of the Frankfurt Parliament in 1848. Parliamentary liberals were willing to compromise and grant funds for the army if the King would make some concessions in return, but this would have meant, to the horror of the right, that basic decisions about the armed might of Prussia would have to be approved by a parliament of lawyers, merchants and civilians who had an increasing ability to attract votes. The lesson was driven home when in late 1861 many left-wing liberals gained seats. Even von Roon lost. Von Roon insisted that Bismarck must be appointed prime minister, because, as he had often said, 'It is better to bleed to death than slowly rot away.' In this way, the famous constitutional conflict began.

The issue was joined when the lower house of parliament rejected the government budget, and proceeded to pass one of its own without including funds for the proposed army reforms. The upper house, whose members were appointed by the king, rejected the latter budget and passed one proposed by the Monarch. The constitution stated that both branches of parliament and the Crown must agree on the budget. Deadlock resulted. The lower house was eager for a compromise, as this would establish the responsibility of the military to the elected representatives of the people. Bismarck would not fall into the trap. He simply ignored the constitution, continued to collect taxes and made no concessions. He begged the question by arguing that since Prussia must survive, it must be governed, even if one unit of the constitutional system disagreed with the budget. Obviously, he would not have argued thus if the king had been that unit. The real question was whether or not Bismarck could continue to collect taxes from an electorate whose representatives had been ignored. The electorate obliged. The Junkers were pleased to discover that they might have their way without parliamentary interference.

Unlike his reactionary colleagues, Bismarck was aware that he could not continue to govern in the face of growing liberal and popular antagonism. If he could demonstrate the superiority of conservative institutions and attitudes to his opponents and to Germans in general, then he might transform parliament into an extension of the royal will. He could not do this by liberal reforms, of course, but if he could divest nationalism of its liberal overtones and transform it into a conservative cause, he might gain overwhelming popular support for old Prussian institutions.

It should be remembered that even after 1848 German liberals had a popular and viable programme for national unification, one that threatened, if successful, to create a united Germany that the right could not control. Chambers of commerce, as well as innumerable associations and congresses of manufacturers, economists, lawyers and merchants, issued constant barrages of declarations and manifestos calling for the gradual and peaceful union of the Germanies. Prussia's customs union, established in 1833, should be extended until a common tariff frontier surrounded all German states. Within each state, liberals should work for constitutional reforms, a common set of political institutions and, finally, interstate negotiations for a federated Germany. Given proper assurances and guarantees, there seemed no compelling reason to expect armed resistance from other European powers. After all, the Italians had had to fight for national unity only because they were subjects of Austria. As for Napoleon III, he saw himself as a sponsor of moderate national unification programmes throughout Europe, and could in any event be appropriately compensated.

Should this programme succeed, Bismarck was well aware that Prussia's influence and her conservative institutions would be mortally threatened. His famous statement that only 'blood and iron', not parliamentary debates, could unify Germany, was not, as is often maintained, the practical view of one who knew the harsh realities of *Realpolitik*. It was a self-fulfilling prophecy: the only policy which, by resting on force, could make national unity seem dependent on the arms of Prussia and the warrior ethic of its ruling élites. Bismarck correctly assumed that nationalism held a higher priority than constitutional reforms even among most liberals. Therefore he used the police and censorship to hold down liberal complaints against his unconstitutional behaviour, while persuading reactionaries that conflict with Austria would be to their advantage.

Foreign policy thus became the means by which Bismarck could forestall domestic reform. In 1864 Prussian troops defeated Denmark and seized lands containing sizeable German populations. Fearing both Prussian aggrandizement and German unity under Prussian leadership, Austria was easily manipulated into war. Bismarck offered assurances to Napoleon III, at the same time giving the Italians a chance to seize territories held by Austria. The Prussian army defeated the Austrians in a few weeks in 1866. The Gerlach brothers were furious at Bismarck's betrayal of the old conservatism. But on the very day of the battle of Königgrätz – the battle that sealed Austria's fate – conservatives tripled their vote in Prussian elections. Those German liberals who had once been so anti-Bismarck now became his admirers. A large group of them formed the National Liberal Party in February 1867, and pledged themselves to support his

22   Bismarck offers the advisory committee of the German parliament the choice between anti-socialist legislation or the dissolution of parliament. Caricature from *Kladderadatsch*, 1884.

'sacred' foreign policy. Indeed, declaring his former actions retroactively constitutional, parliament voted Bismarck a substantial sum. Even though Bismarck's reactionary followers now urged him to abolish parliament, he saw no reason to create antagonism by a *coup* to overthrow men he had learned to manipulate for a conservative programme of national unification through conquest.

The constitution of the newly formed North German Con-federation – as, later, that of the Second Empire – illustrated how Bismarck's dynamic new conservatism could harness modern forces to old Prussian interests. In the new federal parliament the lower house, or Reichstag, would be elected by universal male suffrage, but its ministers would be responsible not to the elected deputies, but to the Chancellor himself. The upper house, or Bundesrat, was so arranged that the will of Prussia would prevail on all crucial matters. As for the dispute over control of the army, Bismarck worked for military budgets free from parliamentary controls. Bismarck's prestige, the insistence of William and his generals, and the knowledge that Bismarck might simply rule without their consent persuaded parliament to settle for long-term military budgets of four and later seven years. Bismarck became an object of public worship when, over an issue which had nothing directly to do with German unification (though his eager press made it seem to), he manoeuvred Napoleon III into the Franco-Prussian War of 1870. In January 1871 William was proclaimed German emperor by an assemblage of princes, aristocrats and generals. The elected representatives of the people were not consulted. They were informed.

The Franco-Prussian War was the first European war in which industrial technology demonstrated its military potential. This and Bismarck's need to satisfy potentially liberal business interests caused him to ignore the complaints of the old right and legislate to favour industrial growth. He removed most guild restrictions on free enterprise, gave state support to the building of railway networks and offered tariff protection to Germany's 'infant' industries. Conservative landowners were not neglected. They gained protection from the competition of cheap imported foodstuffs. After all, landowners pointed out, self-sufficiency in food was necessary for Germany, especially in view of the might of the British fleet. To this, Prussian generals added that the sturdy peasant was a far more dependable recruit than the over-civilized and politically suspect rabble of the cities. When the left-wing liberals in the Reichstag argued that protectionism harmed the ordinary consumer, Bismarck laconically reminded them of the old Lockian principle that the state belonged to the propertied.

Bismarck and the Prussian establishment had no compromises to offer, however, to the Marxist Social Democrats. Not only had the Social Democrats taken up the cause of parliamentary supremacy, but, in theory at least, they were revolutionaries. Worse, after 1880 their votes began to increase dramatically. To Bismarck and the right such men were traitors. Using two attempts on the Emperor's life as an excuse – though neither would-be assassin was a Social Democrat – Bismarck pressured the Reichstag into passing a law against the Social Democrats in 1878. Parliamentarians who sought to protect the civil rights of the left suffered at the polls, though most liberals, mindful of their business connections, had little desire to aid the left. The press, political organizations and meetings of the Social Democrats were outlawed, and their members were harassed. In the hope of attracting workers away from the Marxists, Bismarck once again demonstrated his flexible new conservatism. A series of measures was passed which, through combined state, employers' and workers' contributions, offered some protection to workers against accidents, illness, unemployment and old age. To his amusement, a parliamentary admirer of classical liberalism accused Bismarck of socialism. The Chancellor was pleased to note that, unlike liberal capitalists, the feudal lords of Prussia had always felt an obligation towards their serfs in times of need.

In spite of all his efforts, Bismarck increasingly found himself faced with a parliament that he could not manipulate. Socialist votes continued to increase; indeed, they doubled in 1890. Even the formerly docile liberals were moving leftwards. Bismarck contemplated a *coup d'état*. He could not offer the Marxists anything but suppression; and parliamentary supremacy, looming clearly ahead, would leave the old Prussian élites at the mercy of the masses. Because Germany was a strong and satisfied power, the cry of 'The Fatherland in danger', so often helpful in moving the middle classes to the right in election years, now rang hollow. But there would be no *coup*. In 1888 there was a new Kaiser, William II, who hoped to establish his independence from the man whose immense prestige made him incapable of compromise. There was nothing Bismarck could do. The system he had created made him invulnerable to all Germans but one. In 1890 the Kaiser accepted Bismarck's resignation.

Nevertheless, Bismarck's political legacy remained essentially intact down to 1914 and beyond. In the Reich his successful and conservative alliance of privilege with wealth remained dominant. Germany was ruled by an interchangeable class of aristocrats, generals and bureaucrats. They formed a powerful and united front against the left by co-opting the most influential leaders of heavy industry, energy production and transport and by controlling the bulk of the press. Establishment élites recruited new members almost exclusively from those who shared their traditional outlook. From 1871 to 1914 every chancellor of Germany and two-thirds of all the members of the imperial cabinets were aristocrats. This united 'cartel of fear', as it has been called, held the line against parliamentary supremacy and democratic reforms. Above all, the conservatives feared the main supporters of such changes, the increasingly popular Social Democrats. The latter hoped to break the right-wing monopoly of high office, bring land reform to the great estates, buttress trade unions, increase social welfare programmes and even move towards the nationalization of the means of production.

Bismarck had forged a popular conservative majority by sanctifying traditional Prussian values as the source of German unification. After Bismarck, and with unity achieved, new goals were needed. Threats from the left had to be magnified if rightist élites were to maintain the prestige of Prussian authoritarian militarism against the rising tides of democratic liberalism and international socialism. The 'red menace' had to appear ever more alarming, although the Social Democrats were becoming less revolutionary with each election. The danger of war with France had to be stressed, even though the French desire for revenge was on the wane. New foreign policy goals had to be substituted for Bismarck's drive towards German unity. Correspondingly, industrialists and land-owners (the latter less wholeheartedly) committed themselves to an aggressive foreign policy, and called for a large navy, bigger arms budgets and the pursuit of overseas colonies. Above all, the German establishment and its industrial-based following stressed the need to support the Austrian Empire's continually more feeble attempts to maintain the dominance of the German minority over the Slavic east. Paradoxically, Bismarck's legacy could only be preserved if the new conservative coalition was far more reckless and aggressive than he would have thought wise.

Thus it is not surprising that the Kaiser, his military leaders, his nobles and the leaders of heavy industry constantly emphasized that Germany was destined to become a global power of the same rank as Great Britain or the United States. Leading members of the establishment founded movements like the Pan-Germans, the German Navy League and the German Colonial Society – all pressing for an aggressive German foreign policy. Attracted in considerable numbers to such groups, the lower middle classes gained status in their own eyes by association with political organizations led by some of the most ancient and illustrious names in Germany. When left-wing liberals, trade unionists or socialists complained of heavy arms budgets and demanded social reforms instead, it was commonplace for a chorus of voices on the right to speak darkly of treason and 'red' revolution. As socialist votes continued to increase in the Reichstag, until the Social Democrats became the largest party in 1910, right-

Colonisation.

Deutsche Theorie.

Französische Praxis.

23   While the French massacre their natives, the German carefully tends his colonial plants through league and contribution. Caricature from *Kladderadatsch*, 1884.

wing extra-parliamentary activity flourished. Meanwhile, industrial growth accelerated until Germany was second only to the United States in industrial power, and second to none in arms budgets. Yet the men who ruled this unstable and polarized giant maintained an allegiance to authoritarian, pre-liberal values, and to an aggressive nationalism which most liberals had complacently assumed no longer had any important role to play on what Hegelians used to call the stage of world history.

HEINRICH VON TREITSCHKE

The Bismarckian power-state, or *Machtstaat*, found its most strident and popular expression in the writings of Heinrich von Treitschke (1834–96). Few literate Germans were unacquainted with his *History of Germany* or the many popular articles in which he deified Bismarck and glorified the old Prussian values. The Historiographer Royal of

Prussia, a favourite of William I and Bismarck, Treitschke was a member of the Reichstag from 1871 to 1884 and the intellectual leader of its pro-Bismarck faction. For two decades his lectures at the University of Berlin were attended by the highest ranking members of the government, military and diplomatic establishment. His classes were filled with their sons, members of the right-wing student fraternities, as well as a host of future school-teachers who would help influence the thought of a generation of young Germans. In stark and harsh terms, Treitschke provided the major voice of the new conservatism of the Reich – nationalistic, imperialistic, statist and violently opposed to the left. Treitschke proudly labelled himself a radical reactionary. He dedicated his work to the preservation of the powers of the Prussian throne, the stern virtues of its martial ethic and the subordination of all political goals to German unity and expansion under Prussian leadership.

Englishmen, Treitschke maintained, might delude themselves that 'That government is best which governs least.' Protected by their island from powerful enemies, ruling a global empire of weak, subject peoples, it was easy for Englishmen to think of the state as a necessary evil and nod sagely in agreement with the writings of John Stuart Mill. But where would Germany be if the Great Elector or Frederick the Great had assumed that individual rights were superior to the state's need to survive and grow in the constant crisis of continental politics? Feudal particularism, Treitschke argued, had to be crushed in the eighteenth century; so now, Bismarck must resist liberal individualism. Without the protection of the state there could be no stability or civilized life. But to gain that protection, the individual might even be called upon to sacrifice his life for the collective good, in spite of his alleged right to life, liberty and the pursuit of happiness. Those who believed otherwise needed only to consider Germany's weakness during the Thirty Years War, or when invaded by the armies of Louis XIV and Napoleon. It was, in fact, the historical task of all peoples to build strong nations. Only the unified will of its leaders, a William I or a Bismarck, could decide when the nation faced a state of crisis and what private rights must accordingly be surrendered. Nor, Treitschke held, could the acts of a statesman be subject to the tenets of private morality. What good was the statesman who in time of crisis could say, 'I have told the truth', if that truth destroyed his state?

From the vantage point of his continental cockpit, Treitschke condemned the liberal assumption that the power of the state was gained at the expense of its citizens. On the contrary, the power of the state was the guarantee of the welfare of the individual and the community. Paraphrasing Aristotle, Treitschke asserted that just as a ship an inch long was not a ship because it was too small to row, so also a state was not a state if it was too small to protect its citizens. When Bismarck absorbed smaller states into Prussia and seized Alsace-Lorraine, he acted in accord with the laws of history. Just as matter was ruled by the law of gravity, Treitschke added, so politics was dominated by the law of power. This was why Prussia was uniquely qualified to unite Germany and shape her political institutions. Treitschke agreed heartily with William I's often-quoted remark, 'The German Reich is merely an extension of Prussia.' Unlike the decaying aristocrats of the rest of Europe, Treitschke pointed out, the Prussian noble was imbued with the stern sacrificial virtues of the soldier and the hard discipline of the true servant of the state. The Prussian peasant, more than any class in Europe, had resisted the self-serving arrogance of those who talked of nothing except the rights of man. Although Treitschke feared constitutions as subverting the spirit of communal hierarchy, he grudgingly admitted that the constitutional arrangements of Bismarck did at least allow for the uncontested direction of foreign policy by the royal will.

Treitschke insisted that Bismarck must be granted his 'iron budget', that is, a military budget free from all parliamentary controls. By what right did an electorate ignorant of the great affairs of state, or a collection of middle-class representatives of private interests, presume to have any voice at all in foreign affairs? One of Treitschke's few objections to Bismarck's policies was voiced when universal suffrage was introduced in the Reichstag. Treitschke hoped that this innovation might be reversed, and thanked the God of battles that the system had not been applied to the Prussian parliament. Why should Prussian affairs be given over to any street demagogue who could gain votes by making wild promises of material gain to the masses and encouraging class conflict into the bargain? As for the vaunted increase in literacy and the spread of the daily press, this had merely encouraged every buffoon to think that he had the right to an opinion on complex and crucial matters better left to experts and statesmen. Those who know the popular press of the late nineteenth century would probably agree with Treitschke. What he ignored, however, was the ordinary citizen's need to use the ballot-box to protect his interests against exploitation from above.

Such talk would have been nothing less than socialism to Treitschke; like Bismarck, he wanted the left suppressed by force. Treitschke was quite ignorant of the realities of class and economic life. His attacks on socialism were no more than the vulgar commonplaces of the uninformed reactionary. To him, socialists were merely would-be thieves of property which they were too lazy to earn for themselves. Needless to say, he applauded Bismarck's anti-socialist laws. Treitschke fought long and hard to keep the new study of sociology out of the curriculum of the University of Berlin, for he detested any class analysis of society as divisive and subversive. Sociologists frightened him because they threatened patriotic unity with their analysis of class conflicts, the dominance of élites, the lack of social mobility and the inequities created by advanced and corporate capitalism. To all such social questions, Treitschke had simple answers. History and society were the result of the unfolding of God's will, of which Prussian institutions were the highest expression. This view, often incorrectly attributed to Hegel, was a stand-by of the Prussian right. It enabled conservatives to avoid facing complex problems whose solution might involve reforms at their expense.

Like all Prussian conservatives, Treitschke resented the increased influence of the masses, for this would cause the decay of the traditional moral standards and discipline characteristic, he alleged, of the Prussian character at its best. He feared the social effects of what we would now call the permissive society. Dissatisfied with their material possessions and allotted station in life, the masses would surrender to their innate sensuality and self-indulgence. Treitschke also scorned those social theorists who blamed the criminal's environment for his crime. He insisted that corporal and capital punishment ought to be used more frequently and for a wider variety of crimes. He opposed compulsory elementary education, but thought that it might have some value if used to attack 'moral decay' at its source. Teachers should be recruited from retired non-commissioned army officers whose discipline and influence on the young would serve to repress the 'feminine' softness of the masses.

Treitschke located the moral core of Prussianism in the rural and patriarchal family and village. In the village one found the practice of traditional ways, and the close ties and fixed sense of social role which taught each generation and sex its appropriate functions and mutual obligations. The city, Treitschke remarked, shattered these ties, and stripped the individual of his social identity and consequently of his sense of community and moral character. Treitschke hated Berlin. He was outraged by left-wing politicians who held that women ought to be eligible for higher education and even the vote. Perhaps he sensed that here was a truly revolutionary step, for woman's liberation from her traditional functions would threaten the established hierarchy sacred to the Prussian establishment and its respectable bourgeois following.

Treitschke was no mere defender of the Bismarckian *status quo*. In later life, he supplied the new rationale required to buttress the continuing autocracy of the established élites even after German unification had been achieved. Unlike Bismarck, for example, Treitschke glorified war with arguments going back to Adam Müller. Did it not end the selfish and greedy materialism of liberal individualism, unite all in defence of the community and bring out the heroic in man? Peace, Treitschke believed, mutilated the personality by allowing men to stagnate. Like many traditionalists, Treitschke underestimated the military potential of industrialism and believed that the psychological character of a people was decisive in war. As he put it, cowardly peoples perished; brave peoples expanded. Bismarck, content with German unity and his European power base, disliked imperialist adventures. Treitschke's writings came to be dominated by a crude, bellicose and racist imperialism. Lecturing stridently to his receptive audiences of government and military leaders, he declared that history was nothing but the perpetual struggle of race against race. With a simple-minded and dangerous abandon, he assigned fixed racial characteristics to a wide variety of groups. He insisted, for instance, that orientals were effeminate, blacks natural servants, Jews by nature shylocks, Latins shallow-minded and the Germanic peoples born warriors and state-builders. Because, for Treitschke, state-building was the true vocation of man, this automatically designated the Germanic peoples as superior by virtue of their possession of a truly world-historical destiny.

During election years, Bismarck had on occasion encouraged anti-Semitism as a way of preventing middle-class voters from moving to the left. Treitschke, however, lent the prestige of his name to the intense and violent wave of anti-Semitism which swept Europe during the 1890s. The Jews, he thundered, were responsible for the revolutions of 1848; they controlled the socialist press; their historical rootlessness was such that they were anti-national and un-German. Let them cast off their evil ways, he declaimed, and Germans might tolerate their presence. Treitschke allowed his name to be used on petitions to restrict Jewish immigration, curb Jewish civil rights and set quotas on Jewish participation in government, teaching and law.

Bismarck saw no reason why Slavs should be allowed to rule themselves, but he was too cautious to tie German strength to Austrian weakness and commit Germany to propping up the decaying Habsburg Empire. Treitschke and the various right-wing leagues his work inspired thought it inconceivable that a mighty Germany should ever allow the thinly scattered Germanic stock in the east to be overwhelmed by the vast flood of 'inferior' Slav peasants. Germany, Treitschke warned, must support the Austrian Empire; eastern Europe must remain a German preserve. Even this was hardly enough for him. Germany must contribute its share and more to the ultimate destiny of the white races – a globe dominated by an aristocracy of Teutons and Anglo-Saxons. Should Great Britain prove uncooperative, Treitschke once announced to his students, he would welcome the day when a German army occupied London.

Treitschke's extremely popular views transformed the legacy of Bismarck into far cruder, more reactionary, authoritarian and violent terms than would have been acceptable to the practical-minded master of forceful manipulation towards limited and realistic ends. Indeed, Treitschke's work forms a bridge between nineteenth-century traditionalism and the revolutionary reactionaries of the twentieth century. It is hardly surprising that Treitschke's writings were revived by the German radical right in the 1920s, or that he would be one of the very few nineteenth-century thinkers to win a place in the official Nazi bibliography of required reading.

VII CONSERVATISM UNDER THE THIRD REPUBLIC

The defeat of Napoleon III by Prussia seemed to herald a return of the monarchy in France. Although Léon Gambetta, the republican leader, declared France a republic and sought to wage guerrilla warfare against the Germans, the bulk of the French felt no immediate threat to their interests. Under universal male suffrage, elections were held in February 1871 to form a temporary governing body to negotiate peace terms. Over two-thirds of the deputies returned were royalists with the familiar names of local notables and old aristocratic families. As the party of peace and social order, they moved the government away from radical Paris to Versailles, the traditional home of monarchs. Paris, under siege by Prussian troops, was the last hope of militant Jacobins. The Versailles government angered Parisians by ending the wartime moratorium on rents and debts, thus demonstrating to the lower middle classes of Paris that it held the rights of property more sacred than the suffering of patriots who wanted to continue the war. Tensions mounted when the Versailles traitors, as the Jacobins called them, bought peace from Bismarck by surrendering Alsace-Lorraine and agreeing to pay a huge indemnity. The head of the new government, Adolphe Thiers, sought to disarm the radical National Guard units of Paris, and fighting began among Frenchmen.

Inspired by Robespierre and Proudhon, radicals declared Paris a self-governing commune more out of a sense of isolation than of doctrine. For the Paris Commune was not socialist but Jacobin, contrary to a mythology dear to writers on both the right and the left. The legislation of the Commune respected private property, suspended but did not cancel rent and debt payments, and attacked the powers of the Church. After much suffering as a result of the siege, the Communards were engaged in bloody battles by conservative-minded provincial troops. Defeated in May, thousands of rebels were shot out of hand, while many more suffered slow death in the notorious penal colonies of France.

24 Forged composite photograph depicting the Communard massacre of 62 hostages in the rue Haxo, Paris, on 26 May 1871. The fall of the Commune two days later provoked savage and widespread reprisals from the anti-Communards.

The way now seemed open for the restoration of the monarchy. But the royalist cause was not helped by the demonstration that a government without a king was able and willing to suppress Jacobin radicalism and defend private property by force. Moreover, there were two candidates for the throne. One was the last of the Bourbons, the 81-year-old and childless Comte de Chambord, grandson of Charles X. The other was the young Orleanist Comte de Paris, grandson of Louis-Philippe. Unable to agree on one candidate, the royalist majority supported what seemed a reasonable compromise to political and secular minds. Let Chambord ascend the throne, and name the Orleanist his heir. But Chambord would make no deals. He would rule as Charles X had ruled, and he would never name an Orleanist as his successor. During the Revolution of 1789, the head of the Orleanist family had declared himself Philippe Egalité and had even voted for the execution of Louis XVI. Louis-Philippe himself, furthermore, had betrayed Charles X when he seized the throne without regard for the rights of the Bourbon heir. Finally, Chambord would not be the 'king of the Revolution' and serve under its flag, the tricolour; he insisted upon the white flag of the Bourbons.

In all this he was neither foolish nor stubborn, as is so often remarked; he was behaving as a real king by divine right must behave. No compromise was possible. Dieting heavily so that he might mount his horse and march on Paris in triumph, Chambord slowly waddled off the stage of world history. Distraught royalist politicians sought desperately to prevent the coming Republic. Forcing Adolphe Thiers from office in 1873, they elected Marshal MacMahon as head of government for a seven-year term. Their aim was to stave off the Republic until the death of Chambord left the way open for the Orleanist pretender.

But the heavy campaigning of Léon Gambetta and the restoration of public order led to the victory of an ever higher proportion of republican deputies with each election. In 1875, but only by one vote, constitutional arrangements were passed which would make France a republic. By 1876 republicans outnumbered the combined right of legitimists, Orleanists and Bonapartists by some two to one. Threatened by a permanent republic, and already facing a purge of their extra-parliamentary bastions, the French right forced their version of a Bismarckian constitutional conflict. Ignoring the parliamentary majority, MacMahon dismissed his republican prime minister and appointed a royalist aristocrat in his place in May 1876. The Chamber of Deputies defied him.

The issue was joined. Would France's government be responsible to elected deputies or to an authoritarian president? Unlike Bismarck, MacMahon had no mighty achievements to his credit. Social order was well established. Why should the electorate turn to a substitute monarch? The right was defeated; MacMahon resigned. In 1881 royalists – ultra and moderate alike – were trounced in national and local elections. Republicans promptly began to purge conservatives from army, government and education. It seemed as though the Third Republic could not be undone. Prince Jérôme Bonaparte and the Comte de Paris were anxious to try, but the right now called themselves conservatives, not royalists, and hoped for the emergence of a popular man of the right, a French Bismarck, to lead them in the overthrow of the Republic.

In the late 1880s, many conservatives saw in General Boulanger the needed 'man on horseback'. The General enjoyed great popular fame as the victor in battles fought against the native peoples of Tunis, Algeria and Indochina. He had also distinguished himself against the Prussians in 1870. But Boulanger had supported the Republic and even purged royalists from the military as minister of war under Clemenceau. Still, it was understood that an ambitious political general would have to manoeuvre in ways too devious for a potential monarch, and Boulanger encouraged a certain vagueness about his ultimate intentions. His popularity soared immensely when Bismarck, needing a war-scare in 1887 to push through his military budget, exaggerated a trivial incident with France but backed down when Boulanger ordered partial mobilization. To the ordinary Frenchman, it appeared that at last France had found a champion who might one day restore Alsace-Lorraine. Popularly dubbed 'General Revanche', Boulanger became the object of a powerful personality cult, manifested in hundreds of songs, stories and newspaper articles, and millions of eagerly purchased souvenirs and photographs.

Events favoured Boulanger and those who detested the Republic. In 1886 it had been discovered that Daniel Wilson, son-in-law of the President of the Republic, had sold government appointments, financial secrets and even the prestigious Légion d'honneur to those who could pay the price. A republic recently established among millions of enemies could be mortally threatened by such scandals. The President of France, even though he had no substantial power, made himself ridiculous by clinging to office. The judiciary demonstrated its corruption by acquitting Wilson. Disgust with the Republic raised Boulanger's popularity to new heights. By presenting himself as a potentially strong executive able to override squabbling and corrupt republicans, Boulanger was able to win numerous by-elections to the Chamber under the prevailing system of open candidacies. He saw clearly that real power would be his only if he could mobilize and lead the enemies of the Republic towards a popularly supported *coup d'état*.

In late 1887 Boulanger secretly visited both Jérôme Bonaparte and the Comte de Paris. In return for appropriate assurances, the Orleanist pretender sensed a possible return to power. He placed vast sums and his clerical-royalist press at the disposal of the General. The pretender also issued a manifesto which stated that, if king, he would appoint an upper house to represent the great corporate interests of France, while the lower house would be elected by universal suffrage. Parliament, however, would only advise; the king would have the final say in all matters. Boulanger, presumably, would gain more electoral victories, restore the pretender and play Bismarck to his William. The pretender could hardly be sure that the popular Boulanger would restore the throne, but it was his only hope.

Boulanger now proceeded to win a series of electoral victories. The main points of his programme were that the exiled princes should be allowed to return to France, that there must be a new constitution providing for a powerful executive and that France must return to the stern military virtues and religious faith of her ancestors. To this the General's supporters added a few discreet remarks about lessening the influence of the Jews.

On 27 January 1889 Boulanger's great moment arrived. He defeated the republican candidate in traditionally radical Paris. This was one of the first strong indications that lower middle-class conservatives were becoming a force in urban France. Crowds chanted for Boulanger to seize power and put an end to the Republic. Patriotic leagues of street toughs moved to support the General's cause. To the fury of his supporters, Boulanger lost heart, hesitated and failed to stage the expected *coup*. Many of the republicans in the Chamber had been ready to flee France. Now they trumped up charges against Boulanger and he exiled himself rather than face trial. Some two years later, still in exile, he blew his brains out on the grave of his mistress. In the autumn of 1889 conservatives were once again routed at the polls.

Within three years even the Pope had advised his reluctant supporters to reconcile themselves to the Third Republic. He did so because of the Vatican's fear of the rise of the left. Similarly motivated, many Orleanist large landowners and leaders of finance and industry had already made their peace with the Republic. In turn, the Méline tariff of 1892 heavily rewarded Orleanist business and landed interests. Traditional conservatism seemed doomed in France. Without a king, deserted by the Pope, their would-be strong man an object of ridicule, the old guard watched helplessly as their ranks melted away.

THE DREYFUS AFFAIR

Two events gave a powerful stimulus to the right and proved that the Republic was still vulnerable. One was the Panama scandal; the other

Text in image: PANAMA · WATANA · CUIVRE · MINES D'OR · ALES · PETROLE · CREDIT PROVINC · CONVENT S CELERA · UNION GENERALE · COMPTOIR D'ESCOM · TALMUD · PRIX DE JUSTICE · HAMBOURG · FRANCFORT · BERLIN · PALAIS DES VOLEURS · RANÇAIS! · LE JUIF! VOILA L'ENNEMI! · PRIMERIE SPÉCIALE DU Gde O·· F·· LYON

25 'Frenchmen! The Jew! There is the enemy!' Surrounded by his ill-gotten gains, the Jew in the guise of a ravaging Hydra menaces France. In a coil of the monster's tail Dreyfus can be seen selling information to a German officer. French popular print of the Dreyfus period.

was the most famous trial of the century, that of Captain Alfred Dreyfus. To build a canal at Panama, Ferdinand de Lesseps had collected funds from half a million small investors. The company went bankrupt in 1889. By 1892 an outraged public had forced the Chamber of Deputies to investigate. De Lesseps and his son were sent to prison, and among those who were discovered to have accepted bribes and pay-offs to cover up the company's mismanagement were twelve deputies and senators, five former cabinet ministers, and numerous journalists and newspaper staffs – including that of Clemenceau. The conservative press was swift to point out that the two organizers of the Panama conspiracy were Jewish, Baron Reinach and Dr Herz. Using arguments reminiscent of Burke, de Maistre and Bonald, conservative columnists insisted that elected officials would always be corrupt because bribery and deception were an intrinsic part of the struggle for campaign funds and votes.

Cynicism turned to outrage when, in October 1894, a leading reactionary and anti-Semitic newspaper announced that a Jewish captain serving as a trainee on the General Staff of the French army had been arrested as a German spy. Thus began the notorious Dreyfus affair. It would bring the Republic to the brink of a rightist revolution. It would also forge an alliance between conservatives of the old style and the revolutionary conservatives of the radical right, men who would themselves first gain numbers and impact through the events of the Dreyfus affair.

Agents of army counter-intelligence had discovered that secret information known only to the General Staff had been sold to the Germans. Investigation showed, counter-intelligence claimed, that the handwriting on the incriminating document was that of Captain Dreyfus. In December 1894 a court martial found him guilty, although the defence demonstrated that the handwriting was not similar to his, that the information had not necessarily come from the General Staff, and that Dreyfus had no motive as he came from a wealthy family and was on the threshold of a brilliant career. At this point the Minister of War himself, General Mercier, intervened in the trial to show the judge a dossier of evidence (later demonstrated to be false) which implicated Dreyfus. Mercier would not reveal this evidence to the counsel for the defence as, he claimed, this would endanger national security. Dreyfus was convicted, publicly dishonoured and shipped to Devil's Island. Only much later did it become obvious that Dreyfus had been accused of treason because he was the only Jew on the General Staff. This was evidence enough for the ultra-reactionary counter-intelligence agents of the French army.

Since the 1860s, the French officer class, once the willing tool of Napoleon I, had become dominated by an increasing percentage of officers of noble birth who were royalist, Catholic and closely allied with the Jesuit Order. This 'old-boy' network effectively blocked non-nobles, republicans, Protestants and Jews from advancement. Their racism found a popular response in the wave of anti-Semitism which swept Europe in the 1890s along the path of the westward migration of ghetto Jews fleeing the pogroms of eastern Europe and Russia. To the unsophisticated urban masses, the orthodox appearance and beliefs of the migrants seemed even more alien and threatening than their western co-religionists. Thus ultra-conservatives in France found in the Dreyfus affair a means of attracting extensive popular support for their apparently dying cause through a volatile mixture of ultra-patriotism, revanchism, Catholic royalism and anti-Semitism.

In 1896 an honest counter-intelligence officer, Colonel Picquart, discovered that some of the evidence against Dreyfus had been forged. It also seemed likely that recent leaks of secret information, in handwriting once assumed to be that of Dreyfus, might be coming from the pen of a heavily indebted Catholic officer, Count Esterhazy. The army cleared the Count, but by dubious proceedings. Colonel Picquart was punished for his genuine concern with national security by being posted to a distant and dangerous command. Nevertheless doubts had been raised. On 13 January 1897 Clemenceau's newspaper published Emile Zola's famous *J'accuse*. Zola excoriated the forgeries and lies of the military, and was himself arrested for libel, tried and found guilty without benefit of a thorough airing of his charges. The nation began to split into Dreyfusards and anti-Dreyfusards. Rightist crowds surged through the streets of France howling for death to Zola and the Jews. Learned gentlemen indicated that Zola was only half French (his father was Italian) and that he was an atheistic writer of pornographic books.

To end all doubts, a new and honest Minister of War, Godefroy de Cavaignac, reviewed the evidence, concluded that Dreyfus was in fact guilty and made a speech stressing this to an enthusiastic Chamber of Deputies – a speech posted throughout France. To his mortification, Cavaignac discovered that he himself had been duped by forged documents. A counter-intelligence officer, Colonel Henry,

26   Zola as fire-raiser during the Dreyfus affair. Caricature from the extreme right-wing satirical weekly *Psst . . . !*, 1898.

admitted his guilt and committed suicide in prison. Though they both still believed Dreyfus to be guilty, the Minister of War and the Chief of the General Staff resigned. In February 1899 President Félix Faure died. At his funeral the League of Patriots, led by the radical rightist Paul Déroulède, attempted a *coup*. They pretended to be convinced, without evidence, that the anti-Dreyfus President had been poisoned by Jews to aid Dreyfus and Germany. The new President, Emile Loubet, now aware that the Republic itself was threatened, arranged for a retrial of Dreyfus in the same year. More or less ignoring the evidence on the assumption that army prestige, national security and conservative values demanded it, the military judges once again found Dreyfus guilty. For the second time, General Mercier had intervened. He lied under oath by testifying that he had seen a secret document in which the Kaiser himself had implicated Dreyfus and in writing. Unfortunately, Mercier continued, the court could not view the document as the Kaiser had threatened war should it be revealed. President Loubet finally put an end to the farce and pardoned Dreyfus. Ultimately, in 1906, Dreyfus was cleared of all charges by a civilian court. He went on to win the Légion d'honneur for exceptional bravery in the 1914–18 war.

It seems clear and simple now, but at no time during the Dreyfus affair did the public have the least notion of the most elementary facts. The French press was unbelievably partisan. The wildest rumours were printed as sober truth. The conservative press, which had by far the largest readership, also had the strongest need to deceive – which it did with relish. The primary source of information was the army itself, busily forging documents and leaking 'information' to such characters as Edouard Drumont. His book, *La France juive* (1886), was the most notorious anti-Semitic tract in modern history. Drumont used his extremely popular newspaper, *La Libre Parole*, to disseminate 'evidence' which he himself often manufactured.

All this he did with a clear conscience. Whether Dreyfus was guilty or innocent was not the point. Drumont argued that Jews were traitors by nature and that the army was all that stood between France and the Prussians, and must be defended at all costs. Ordinary minds were further confused by rightist intellectuals, such as Maurice Barrès, who insisted that only diseased Teutons like the philosopher Kant could imagine that there was some universal standard of justice which ought to apply even when a nation's survival was at stake. As for the left, Barrès declared, they did not know whether Dreyfus was innocent, but they did know that they could use the 'little Jew' to destroy all that was great and traditional in France: the Church, the army, the aristocracy and authority itself.

Drumont was able to appeal to the unsophisticated minds of the newly literate masses by using a crude Darwinian racism and claiming for it the prestige of science. According to Drumont, the Dreyfus case was just one part of a conspiracy of international Jewry against France. When Bertillon, the handwriting expert who had originally incriminated Dreyfus, was forced to admit that the handwriting actually resembled that of Count Esterhazy, Drumont calmly explained that a Jewish syndicate must have hired experts to train Dreyfus in forgery. The general hysteria was immense. When rumours spread that a Jewish fleet was on its way to liberate Dreyfus, security was reinforced by the nervous guards on Devil's Island.

27–28 Anti-Dreyfusard caricatures from *Psst . . . !*, by Forain. Left, German militarism and Jewish interests behind Zola's defence of Dreyfus, 1898. Right, the Jew steps to power over the corpse of France, 1899 (during the retrial of Dreyfus).

The Church was overwhelmingly committed to the army. The Church hierarchy was dominated by the reactionary Assumptionist Fathers who had long made a practice of holding public Masses to do penance for the sins of the Revolution of 1789. Had not the wrath of God been visited on France's secular liberalism by Bismarck's troops and the 'red' Communards? In the spirit of de Maistre and Bonald, the editors of the Assumptionist paper, *La Croix*, called for a restoration of the old unity of throne and altar. They also insisted that Dreyfus was part of an international conspiracy bent upon weakening the French army and seizing France's territories. The Jesuit Order called for political and economic sanctions against Jews and publicly expressed hope for the day when they might be banished from Europe altogether. The Secretary of State of the Vatican urged all Catholics to denounce Dreyfus. Comte de Mun, the leading French Catholic intellectual and deputy, one who had ceased being a legitimist only because the Pope had so commanded in 1892, denounced the 'Jewish conspiracy' in the Chamber. So also did the Premier, Jules Méline, who, though he was a republican, hoped to forge an alliance with the right against socialism and saw the Dreyfus affair as one means of doing so.

Until the 1880s, ultra-patriotic nationalism in France had been associated with the Jacobinism and liberal reforms of the armies of the Revolution and Napoleon. The French right, unlike the Prussian right, could hardly claim a monopoly of warrior virtues. The Dreyfus case helped reverse this. French conservatives portrayed an image of patriotic generals who, in the name of French national security, refused to clear themselves of the charges of traitors. When it was proved that Colonel Henry had forged documents, Charles Maurras, the intellectual leader of the French right, pointed out that if one permitted a soldier to kill for France one could hardly label forgery for the same noble purpose a crime. Drumont raised a subscription for the widow of Colonel Henry. The letters he received indicated a powerful and popular belief that the Germans, the English, and above all the Jews, were out to use Dreyfus to destroy France.

The letters came, in general, from military officers, aristocrats, royalist notables, priests, religious orders and small businessmen. Those who provided the funds often insisted that the Jewish traitors of France ought to be burned, impaled, drowned or shot. During the Dreyfus case, defending the army, the Church and the purity of

French blood became a popular cause, and conservatives now found a new means of eroding the democratic egalitarianism established by the Revolution of 1789. France was jolted to the right. The streets of the cities and larger towns were dominated by ultra-patriotic military leagues. Led by retired military officers and young nobles, the leagues were joined or supported by mobs of shopkeepers, clerks, artisans, butchers, packing-house workers and sales personnel. Fresh from huge protest meetings, mobs would often beat Jews and plunder their shops. The French in Algeria were singularly vicious; here militant racism was encouraged by the direct benefits of imperialist conquest.

Traditional conservatives were quick to see the opportunity offered by an alliance with the radical right. The Orleanist pretender swiftly allied himself with the leaders of the rightist crowds. He urged his followers to join the patriotic leagues, and hoped to benefit from Déroulède's attempted *coup* at the funeral of President Faure. But the army did not move. Had there been massive economic dislocation or war, then the Third Republic might have fallen. In the event there were only incidents, as when the pro-Dreyfus President of the Republic was severely beaten in public by men who possessed some of the most famous names of aristocratic France. When Dreyfus was pardoned and the Republic was once again secure, the republicans proceeded to take revenge on the right. French conservatives were extremely vulnerable, not so much because they had allied themselves with militarism and racism, but because they had so gleefully attached themselves to fraud.

THE COUNTER-ATTACK OF THE REPUBLICANS

Led first by Waldeck-Rousseau and then by Emile Combes, the republicans purged royalists and devout Catholics from state and army. The Church's activities during the Dreyfus affair convinced republicans that the clergy was the very source of reaction. The Assumptionist Order was abolished, as were thousands of Catholic schools, charities and hospitals. Religious orders lost their right to teach. Thousands of embittered priests and nuns fled into exile. Pius X retaliated by punishing bishops who supported the Republic. The French broke diplomatic relations with the Vatican, and in 1905 passed a Law of Separation which confiscated Church property and lent it out to rigorously supervised associations of laymen. Though compromises were often forced by local counter-attacks of the faithful, the Church lost state support and secular privileges. By 1906, when the right was again heavily defeated at the polls, the army seemed humbled and France close to dechristianization. Civil marriages and the number of unbaptized children rapidly increased. Recruits to the priesthood were few and mediocre. In growing numbers, the young were attending secular schools whose teachers were militant republicans.

It seemed that now, finally, the new government of Clemenceau could leave behind the ancient struggles of clerics versus anti-clerics, so characteristic of the pre-modern left and right, and concern itself with the social problems generated by industrialism. It was not to be. With the Republic secured, the Radical Republicans, or Radicals as they were oddly called, concentrated on the sheer defence of the property rights of their millions of supporters. The Radicals dominated politics until the war. Although Germany and Great Britain had already begun to construct the modern welfare state, France did not. The labouring poor were not helped, even though profit rates increased and real wages declined.

Not surprisingly, trade unionism and socialism grew apace. The number of strikes and workers involved in strikes (including white-collar workers) increased fivefold. The years from 1892 to 1910 were the most militant in the history of the French working class. Most strikers simply wanted to improve their wages, hours and working conditions. But many workers were led by revolutionary syndicalists who ignored the rules of liberal capitalism and sought to bring down the government itself by massive general strikes. Clemenceau ignored the difference and used the police and the army to support businessmen and strike-breakers in conflicts with workers. There had been 52 Socialist deputies in 1906; by 1914 there were 103. They were now the second largest party in France – the Radical Republicans held 136 seats. It seemed as though the Socialists might soon gain control of parliament and perhaps make good their demand for the national-ization of the means of production. The fears of the right may be imagined; even the Communards had believed in private property. Right-wing and moderate republicans began to unite with the remnants of the traditionalists. In France, conservatism increasingly came to mean the defence of the rights of private property owners against the left.

VIII THE RISE OF THE RADICAL RIGHT
1890–1914

By the turn of the century, increasing numbers of traditional French conservatives realized that they must either surrender their values, become merely defenders of capitalism or turn to the radical right. Their followings had been steadily eroded by the sweep of industrialism, the gains of liberal democracy and the increasing support for the left. The right had lost all elections since 1885. Consequently, any hope for a return to pre-liberal principles rested on the revolutionary potential of ultra-patriotic and royalist leagues. The most important of these was the Action Française.

Founded in the violent 'Dreyfus' summer of 1899, the Action Française soon came under the leadership of the prolific writer, Charles Maurras. He was to remain the dominant intellectual popularizer of the right down to and during the Second World War. Among others, the novelist Maurice Barrès helped Maurras bring a new intensity, violence and brutality to ideas derived in large measure from earlier conservatives. From the start the founders of the Action Française declared it to be neither another political party nor an academic school of philosophy. It was, they insisted, a conspiracy to create a state of mind in the French public which would culminate in a conservative revolution to restore pre-modern values and institutions: a revolution which, as Maurras put it, ought to be brought about 'by any means necessary, even legal'. The goal of 'integral nationalism', as it has been called, was to intensify the passions and hatreds generated by popular nationalism and to direct the energies thus released to the support of a wide range of ultra-conservative principles.

It has been said that Maurice Barrès had more impact on French intellectuals than any other person during the decade of nationalist revival just prior to 1914. A Boulangist deputy in 1889, Barrès had founded and led a variety of ultra-patriotic groups, and had participated in the abortive *coup* of the anti-Dreyfusards in 1899. In his novel of 1897, *Les Déracinés*, Barrès broke completely with the rational and cosmopolitan thought of the Enlightenment. Indeed, he

Avant.

29   The peasant's lot before and after the Revolution of 1789. Anti-Semitic caricature from *Psst . . . !*, by Caran d'Ache, 1898.

Aujourd'hui.

broke with conscious thought altogether. Frenchmen, he asserted, should not use rational calculation to decide what France ought to be; instead they should immerse themselves in the deepest levels of their subconscious instincts. In these instincts they would discover what France was and must be: a living reality whose nature must be determined by the collective experience and responses bred in French blood and soil by generations of ancestors. Bonald and de Maistre had counselled men to follow the customs which their ancestors had formed through centuries of practical experience; Barrès insisted that true Frenchmen, if uncorrupted by the liberal rationalism of the Enlightenment, must feel, think and act in ways similar to the generations of dead they had replaced.

Accordingly, there could be no international standards of abstract truth. For the French, there could only be French truth, French reason and French justice. Truth was what was good for the nation. Barrès denounced liberals who ceaselessly discussed every public question in the light of a mythology that clung to the absurd fictions of objective mind and absolute truth. Truth was always relative to a situation and forged by emotional needs. In this sense, Barrès argued, France was ruled by foreigners, because, whatever their ancestry, republican liberals denied the instincts and intuitions which defined what was French and what was not. Borrowing a notion from Nietzsche, Maurras added that French liberals, like Socrates, deserved the hemlock because they cynically employed superficial reasoning to deprive the French masses of the deep and unanalysed truths of their ancient, inherited and instinctive attitudes and behaviour. Rational thought had become the enemy of community customs, solidarity and action.

Maurras and Barrès agreed that Dreyfus, having no French roots, would easily become a traitor even if he were not one now. If by any chance he were innocent of the specific acts charged, no matter, for French justice must heed only that which was good for France. The army, once committed, must be upheld. A native of Lorraine, Barrès was well aware that only the military could restore the lost provinces.

Vente — Achat — Échange

30   The intellectual sells his Christianity to the Jew. Anti-Semitic caricature from *Psst . . . !*, 1898.

Why should the community be required to put the rights of any individual above its survival? What about the rights of those buried in the military cemeteries of France? – where Barrès liked to wander and contemplate the eternal return of blood to soil. The community, Barrès concluded, owed nothing to those who were alien in fact or spirit to its ancient ways. Through Barrès and others, the Action Française and the radical right learned to make use of the new theories of social behaviour which emphasized the irrational forces of instinct, intuition and the subconscious.

From the Enlightenment to the middle of the nineteenth century, nearly all the great intellectual creations of the West had tended to buttress and universalize the ideology of middle-class liberalism: Newtonian science, classical political economy, deism in religion, Romantic individualism, and the analysis of human nature itself through associationist psychology. The study of history began to reverse this trend by teaching men to eschew universal norms and to try to judge the past on its own terms. But it was the enormous impact of social Darwinism – oversimplified and popularized – that gave ultra-conservatives their first chance to mount an intellectual counter-offensive; a thrust bolstered by the sure sense that their arguments coincided with the latest scientific views on the nature of man as forged by the dynamics of evolution. Barrès, Maurras and the radical right welcomed this sober basis for the otherwise irrational mystique of blood and soil. The work of the great biologist seemed to sanction the view that the 'most favoured races' (to use Darwin's phrase) had evolved through centuries of struggle for limited means of survival. Traditional conservatives often refused to believe that man had not sprung full-blown from a unique act of divine creation, or that he was not born to fulfil the transcendent and ideal purposes of his creator through the grand drama of salvation. The new radical conservatives, however, were pleased to hear that man was only a superior species of animal, who, favoured by accidental variations, had clawed his way to dominance from his origins in a fortuitous combination of chemicals in the primeval slime. While there were also ways in which liberals and the left could put Darwinism to ideological uses, Darwinism in its most literal application favoured the heroic vitalists of the ultra-right and their theories of race and heredity.

Those who wished to defend the absolute right of private property and denounce social reform gained similar support from the enormously popular ideas of Herbert Spencer. According to Spencer, just as free enterprise produced the best and cheapest products in the long run, so too the struggle for survival, if unmitigated by weak-minded humanitarianism, produced those who achieved most. For the nationalistic right of continental Europe, social Darwinism did away with the need for complex moral judgments about the relative values of cultures, societies and institutions. Survival became the only criterion for nations and races; what was best for France, for Germany, for Aryans or for Slavs was that which promoted their expansion at the expense of those who, if they could not prevent it, demonstrated that they were indeed 'unfit'. Thus the politics of 'blood and iron' led to the ideology of blood and soil; and both seemed to derive from science at its best. The left, too, could be denounced in the name of the new science of biology, for both liberal humanitarianism and socialist internationalism seemed subversive of the prior need of nation or race for disciplined and militant unity.

The Franco-Prussian War of 1870 was the first conflict to be interpreted in Darwinian terms. Both Prussians and Frenchmen drew appropriate conclusions. Had not Prussia prevailed because she knew the value of patriotic collectivism, class unity and authoritarian guidance from above? After the Dreyfus affair and until the Republic proved its capabilities in the First World War, the French right insisted that republican democracy and left-wing theories of class reinforced those weaknesses which ultimately caused nations and races to succumb in the struggle for survival. Indeed, if one abandoned careful reasoning and complex social analysis, as social Darwinism encouraged, the possibilities were endless. Barrès and Maurras refused to blame French capitalists, industrialists, landow-ners, or the intricate structures of corporate capitalism, for France's recurring economic crises. The Action Française much preferred to single out for blame foreign interests, immigrant workers, Jews or international bankers. Thus racist nationalism enabled the radical right to ally itself with business interests, counter the left's demand for social reform and focus social discontent on a variety of 'aliens'.

Throughout the West during these years, anthropologists and their popularizers bombarded the public with simple equations between achieved levels of civilization and innate racial characteristics. Were not European nations more powerful, their populations more literate and their cultural achievements far superior to the tribal and peasant populations of the non-West? Scales of racial capacity were propounded in solemn tones, with Caucasians to be found at the upper levels, and blacks or aborigines just above the great apes. Liberal imperialists assumed that subject peoples might be civilized by contact with the West. Conservative imperialists argued that innate racial differences could never be changed. Thus conquest and permanent exploitation seemed fair enough. The French right, however, wished to reconquer Alsace-Lorraine before concentrating upon overseas diversions. Barrès himself argued that in spite of 1870 the Teutons were an inferior race. We have already heard the grandiose claims of Treitschke. The popular press was full of heroic tales of nation- and empire-building, heavy with Darwinian symbolism. It is not surprising that the European masses greeted the onset of the First World War with some degree of enthusiasm.

No nation was too liberal or too Christian to be impressed by late nineteenth-century racist imperialism. In the United States, the Reverend Josiah Strong in his best-seller, *Our Country* (1885), argued that the Protestant Anglo-Saxon 'race' of North America represented the purest and, therefore, most militant form of Christianity. When the final competition for scarce lands arrived, Anglo-Saxon Christians would bear witness to the survival of the fittest and join with other Christian nations in dominating the lesser breeds of savage idolators. It is no coincidence that variations on this theme became popular in the United States as the flood of Irish, Slav and Italian peasantry poured into the cities of the eastern seaboard. American nativism and 'Americanism' seethed among small-town Protestant Anglo-Saxon stock, especially as the poverty-stricken new arrivals inevitably became ghetto-dwellers with the highest rates of unemployment, destitution and crime. Worse, they often had swarthy complexions, spoke in strange tongues, professed religious allegiance to the Vatican and did not respect the upright Puritan ethic. To the further discomfiture of the American right, big-city wardheelers often corraled the votes of the new citizens for the Democratic Party, while the immigrants themselves were able to infuse new life into the otherwise moribund American left. Unlike Europe, however, ethnic hatreds were held relatively in check in the United States. This was not simply because of the dominance of the liberal tradition there; it was also the result of the sheer number of immigrants. Against so many millions there could be segregation and

THE INEVITABLE RESULT TO THE AMERICAN WORKINGMAN OF INDISCRIMINATE IMMIGRATION.

31 Caricature from *Judge*, New York 1892. During the decades 1880–1900 immigration to the United States reached nearly 8 millions and was increasingly concentrated in the large cities of the East.

discrimination, but the massive and brutal destruction that Europe was to witness in the twentieth century was out of the question.

Relative to the general population in western Europe, the Jews were few in number, high in status and extremely visible in those sectors of society most threatening to the right. Barrès and Maurras were well aware of this. Indeed, in 1898, the year of Zola's *J'accuse*, Barrès campaigned for the Chamber as an anti-Semite. He lost partly because his opponent accused him of being soft on the issue and himself campaigned with the simple slogan of 'Death to the Jews'. During the Dreyfus affair, Maurras's editorials offered a deal to the agitated crowds: give France a king, and he will give you the Jews. Edouard Drumont, as we have seen, was France's leading anti-Semite. He was also a supporter of the Action Française and a propagandist for a wide range of ultra-conservative issues. The Jew,

Drumont declared, had no roots in the soil; how could he do anything except go wherever profit led him? When the Jacobins freed the Jews in the Revolution of 1789, they had created a nation of enemies within France. It was easy, Drumont added, for rich Jews to corrupt republican deputies who had little wealth and no enduring status. But a monarch, the army, the aristocracy, the great landed proprietors, the Church – were not these invulnerable? The Jews only supported republicanism as a means of gaining control of France. They knew that traditional institutions stood in their way. Was not the leading anti-cleric and republican the 'Jew', Léon Gambetta? 'Jewish' liberalism, Drumont continued, was simply an attack on the true France of discipline, authority and duty. It was Jewish capitalists who exploited the honest workers of France, even while Jewish socialists called for Frenchman to rise against Frenchman in an international class struggle. Let the Jews be warned, concluded the Action Française. In the end all Frenchmen would unite to destroy them.

Naturally enough, the Action Française and other patriotic leagues looked to the army. There was the power to topple the Republic, defeat the Germans and remodel France along authoritarian lines. Barrès hoped for the emergence of a stronger Boulanger, although the Action Française was committed to a restoration of monarchy. Maurras and Barrès were furious when French politicians refused to back the army to the hilt in Algeria and Indochina. With Georges Sorel, a later convert to royalism who was to influence Mussolini, the leaders of the Action Française admired violence whatever its inspiration or goal. They saw violence as an act of purification which raised men above their mundane self-concerns. Thus the warrior or the violent revolutionary – left or right – was superior to the complacent, peace-loving, manipulative bourgeois – republican, prudent, moderate and cowardly. Who, Sorel asked, ran the French political system? A group of lawyers whose sole function was to negotiate favours for their powerful *nouveaux riches* clients at the expense of the community.

The radical right in France admired the Church, but not simply out of religious conviction. The clergy was one of the bastions of reaction. Catholicism upheld the most ancient values of France. Like the army, the Church enjoyed an authoritarian structure based on discipline and submission. In the first decades of the twentieth century, the vast majority of French bishops supported the Action

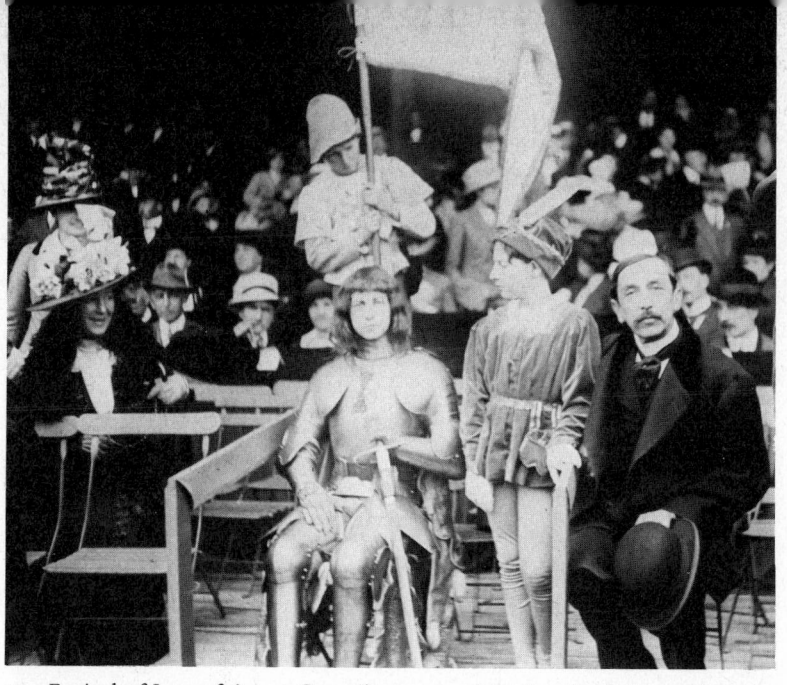

32 Festival of Joan of Arc at Compiègne, 1913. Maurice Barrès is seated on the right. Beatified in 1909, Joan of Arc became the cult-figure of the radical right in France.

Française. Sorel pointed out that liberals must always oppose the Church because its ancient teachings and rituals contradicted all that seemed reasonable to men of science and enlightenment. But the Church was the living proof of the superficiality of rational thought. For centuries the Church had commanded the faith, power and even violence of the masses with its irrationalities of dogma and ritual. That, Sorel argued, in the spirit of de Maistre, was what liberals could not forgive; for what comparable enduring structure had pure reason built? What passion and energy had ever been attracted to liberal ideologies?

Barrès and Maurras did have difficulties with the Vatican. Barrès suspected its internationalism. Maurras, as he put it, could hardly be expected to believe in the gospel according to four obscure Jews. His publicly professed atheism forced the Pope to place his works on the Index for a time. But the leaders of the Action Française, unconcerned with 'bourgeois' standards of absolute truth, were eager to uphold those myths which motivated conservatives and fed the 'will to power' of the right. The doctrines of the Church were useful to that end. At the Institute of the Action Française, the *Syllabus of Errors* of Pius IX formed an important part of the curriculum. The students of the Institute helped to promote the sacred legend of the new cult-figure of the nationalistic right, Joan of Arc; in 1908 a professor at the Sorbonne who questioned her divine credentials was severely beaten. Royalist partisans often shouted down liberal or Jewish professors. Indeed, until 1914 the student organizations of the radical right dominated the Latin Quarter.

Unlike conservatives in central Europe, the French right by 1890 could hardly deny that the principles of 1789 were themselves an integral part of the national tradition. During the Revolution itself, Burke, de Maistre and Bonald had stressed that Europe was witnessing an eruption against all that was truly French, but with each decade this became less credible. Maurras resorted to sheer insult, inspired by the ideas of the well-known and reactionary historian, Hippolyte Taine, for whom the Revolution of 1789 was simply an outburst of the bestial passions of a mob of maniacs.

Maurras did not dwell on the Revolution. He preferred, sensibly enough, to stress the weaknesses of the heritage of 1789 as revealed in the parliamentary politics of the Third Republic. With Sorel he castigated the republican politicians. Could they ever be anything but vote-seeking pimps skilled at masking fraudulent deals with egalitarian rhetoric? How could the presidents and ministers of the Republic possibly speak for France? They presided over a fragmented multi-party system which necessarily produced weak coalition governments subject to constant paralysis by deputies who were themselves little more than the prisoners of parochial interests. Indeed, France had had 42 different governments from 1885 to 1914, and their policies reflected the usual results of endless compromises. Perhaps frustrated by his own series of electoral defeats, Barrès hoped that a 'man of the nation' would smash the Republic in the name of France. Maurras would have settled for this but he preferred a king. He feared that even a strong man would need to pander to the masses to consolidate his rule, whereas one chosen solely by the mysteries of genetic fiat could rule above all parties, constituencies and ordinary political limits. The Orleanist pretender agreed, and he urged his supporters to donate money and energies to the Action Française. He himself retained a certain royal aloofness from a group he could not control outright.

The man who set the social policies for the Action Française was the Comte de la Tour du Pin, revered by Maurras as the 'master'. La Tour was a legitimist from a family which had suffered much from 1789. Like his brilliant contemporary, the sociologist Emile Durkheim, La Tour feared that societies based on liberal individualism and egalitarianism frustrated man's deepest need, a sense of communal belongingness. Isolated and alienated, modern man faced a bleak and frightening future because all protective sub-groups, including finally the family, would collapse. Correspondingly, La Tour revived the old conservative vision of an organic corporate society in which each Frenchman would belong to a guild or corporation appropriate to his work, profession or status. Each corporate body would have broad powers of self-regulation, including the power to tax its members and use the resulting funds to protect them against accidents, ill-health, unemployment and old age.

Maurras hoped that this social programme would attract workers away from trade unionism and socialism, and end the power of the voting masses. La Tour's plan called for voting by order, rather than head, within each corporation – a throwback to the pre-revolutionary Estates General. Moreover, La Tour included the representatives of ancient families among corporate voters, dividing the rest into separate orders of owners, managers and workers. This meant that the workers would be in a permanent minority. The Chamber of Deputies would be replaced by a Chamber of Corporations; even this institution would possess the power only to advise the monarch. It is not surprising that the industrial proletariat was highly under-represented among the supporters of the Action Française.

Pope Leo XIII adopted some of La Tour's ideas in his famous encyclical of 1891, *Rerum Novarum*. Often described as a progressive approach to the problems of modern industrialism, the encyclical was in fact a call for the return to medieval Christian principles. It is true that capitalists were violently denounced for their ruthless exploitation of the workers. But the principle of private property was defended as part of God's natural order, and workers were told that they must neither strike nor heed the revolutionary rantings of socialists. Did not scripture reveal that men must suffer, labour and humbly follow in the bloodstained footsteps of Christ? The Pope recommended two ways to help the workers. The medieval guild system must be restored to shield all from the destructiveness of unlimited competition; and the lands, powers, wealth and controls over education taken from the Church must be returned. Only then would the Church have the authority and the means to carry on the mighty work of Christ and apply once again the principles of Christian brotherhood to society. Truly Christian capitalists would not exploit their workers, and the latter, with dignity and faith restored, would be invulnerable to the militants of the left. In the Chamber of Deputies the Comte de Mun and a small group of Social Catholics tried to legislate some small portion of the social programme of the right, but to little effect. Outside the Chamber, the shock troops of the right acted as strike-breakers and scabs, as the financial backers of a variety of ultra-conservative groups intended. Maurras condemned strikes, especially in heavy industry, as a betrayal of the social cohesion and military power needed to face the enemy across the Rhine.

The Action Française and other nationalist leagues drew their support from aristocrats, military officers, clergy, members of the religious teaching orders banned by the Republic, upper middle-class industrialists (especially those in war-related industries), small shopkeepers and, finally, villagers from traditionally royalist areas. Their strength increased with each international crisis, and as the war grew nearer a wave of ultra-nationalism swept over the supporters of the right, especially the urban lower middle classes. In 1912 Raymond Poincaré became premier; he was elected president in 1913. The Action Française approved. Here was a man who assumed that war was inevitable, urged Russia to meet the German challenge by force of arms and held all the appropriate conservative attitudes on domestic questions, even though he did believe in republican institutions.

The slaughter of 1914–18 brought Barrès's glorification of the dead and his cult of sacred violence to the fore. In speech and essay, he proclaimed France's religious duty to fight in what was nothing less than a holy struggle. On the sacred soil of Verdun, he declared, Frenchmen were regenerated even as they raised their bloody hands in death; with such soldiers the spirit of all the ancient dead was raised in a mystic celebration of the Mass. Their shattered bodies, Barrès intoned, were the ultimate proof that France, though she had once broken with the great traditions of the old régime, had nevertheless

remained true in spirit to her past. In short, during the war Barrès
spoke with the voice of blood, soil and sacred violence in the cause of
reaction. Later we shall hear that voice again, in harsh Teutonic
cadences.

Of all the European states, only the Austrian Empire depended for
its very survival on the success of ultra-conservatism. In Metternich's
day, traditional conservatism could still hold the line against
liberalism and Slav nationalism. By the end of the century, however,
economic modernization and Slav ethnic consciousness had created
sweeping challenges to the continued dominance of the German
minority. Ultimately, this minority could only hope to maintain its
privileged status and power by thrusting aside the moderate
traditional conservatism of the Habsburgs, and replacing it with the
crude and harsh extremism of the racist and authoritarian ultra-right.
Thus there arose in Austria the most strident and popular radical
right-wing social movements that Europe was to see before the days
of Mussolini and Hitler.

Elsewhere in Europe nationalism had created unified peoples loyal
to their governments; this and industrial growth were the twin
sources of strength and great-power capability in the latter decades of
the nineteenth century. In the Austrian Empire, however, nationalism and industrialism had the opposite effects. Industrialism
pulled the Slav peasant away from his kinship groups and local ties,
and thrust him into town, factory and white-collar posts. There he
competed with entrenched Germans for jobs, housing and schooling.
Combined with growing literacy, this created a sense of Slav ethnic
identity and national potential, and an awareness of German
exploitation. Increasingly, the more modernized of the Slav peoples,
especially the Bohemians, began to agitate for equal rights or even
autonomy within the Empire.

For a brief period, in the 1860s, the German Austrians had shown
liberal tendencies. Once they had gained a parliament (dominated by
the propertied), however, and after some anti-clerical and *laissez-faire*
economic legislation, they began a rapid drift to the right. They
feared that democracy would erode German power, and parliament
in Vienna was already rendered unworkable by ethnic hatreds. The

Habsburg rulers were also faced with inherent contradictions in the Empire which could not be resolved, although they could be ignored. If they supported German dominance, they would antagonize their Slav subjects; if they made concessions to the Slavs, they would infuriate the Germans. To stimulate industrial growth would be to increase ethnic consciousness until the Empire was torn apart. To remain backward would mean that the Empire would exist only so long as the great powers found it convenient.

In 1859 Italy won her freedom with French help. In 1867 Hungary gained considerable autonomy as a result of Prussia's defeat of Austria. By the end of the century and with the aid of that other multi-national anachronism, Russia, Czech and Serb nationalism threatened the very core of the Empire. There was no realistic way to force the haphazard provinces of the Habsburgs into the mould of a modern nation state. There were many, notably the Austrian socialists, who hoped that concessions to the Slav peoples would lead to a federated but strong empire of co-equals. But it was difficult to imagine concessions as doing more than feeding the desire for full independence. The Habsburgs continued to alternate between repression and conciliation in the traditional manner. But the bulk of the Austro-German middle classes increasingly demanded the use of force against the Slavs in order to preserve the Empire and German supremacy within it.

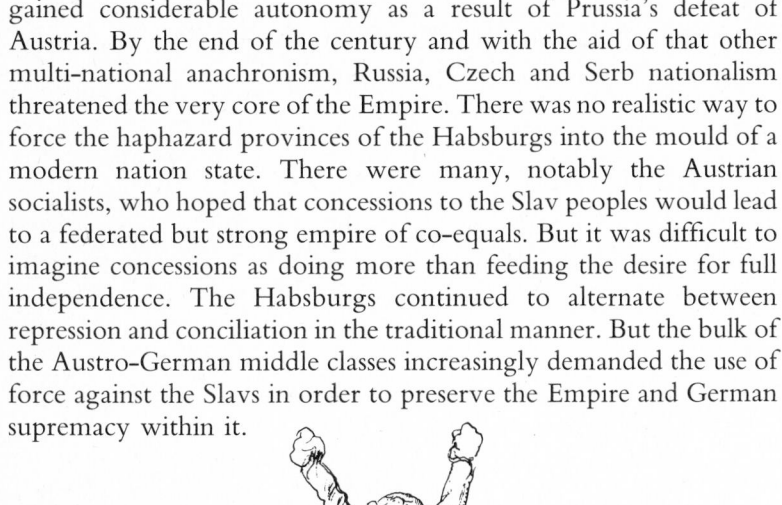

33 'The Czech when he first comes to Vienna and when he grows roots.' A typically vicious anti-Slav caricature from the Viennese satirical weekly *Figaro*, 1899.

The first to capitalize on this right-wing surge of the Austro-Germans was Georg von Schönerer, who founded his Pan-German Party in 1885. The titled son of a railway magnate, Schönerer started as a liberal in the Austrian parliament, but moved to the right as democracy, socialism and Slav nationalism threatened German property, jobs and power. Leading an already established Pan-German movement, he proposed the following programme: Throw out the weak and pro-Slav Habsburgs and unite (Anschluss) with the Hohenzollern German Reich to gain the numbers and power to subjugate the Slavs permanently. Break with the Catholic Church and adopt Lutheranism which, Schönerer believed, reinforced the discipline and martial qualities of the Prussian. Legislate to protect the small farmer from Jewish money-lenders, and the small shopkeeper from the Jewish big retailer. Protect the guilds, suppress the socialists, remove the Jews from their professions of high status and prestige and drive them back to the ghettos. Finally, Schönerer insisted that throughout the Empire the rights and powers of the German minority must be reinforced in every way. To accomplish all this, Schönerer advocated, of necessity, an authoritarian state committed to what Treitschke had called the eternal race struggle between Slav and German. As the decade progressed, Schönerer spat out his proposals in brutal harangues to ever larger and more spellbound crowds of middle-class German Austrians.

When in 1897 the Premier, Count Badeni, made Czech as well as German an official language of the imperial bureaucracy, Schönerer's popularity rose dramatically. How dared the Habsburgs betray German culture by forcing their loyal civil servants to learn the complex language of an inferior race of peasant upstarts? Many of Schönerer's followers were state employees or white-collar workers who had struggled from poverty to marginal status and income. In Badeni's ordinance they sensed the ultimate danger of the awakening of the Bohemian peasant masses. Prague had been overwhelmingly German in 1856; by 1890 it was overwhelmingly Czech. Economic modernization brought with it rural migration to the cities and ever greater competition between Czech and German. Significantly, where Germans and Czechs mingled, as in the Sudetenland, there were often massive demonstrations and riots when jobs were assigned, schools built or neighbourhoods desegregated. Badeni's ordinance brought the German middle classes into the streets. They were often supported by Catholic artisans who feared competition from the Jewish craftsmen flooding in from the east, and by workers who had deserted socialism because, as Schönerer pointed out, only the Pan-Germans would defend their jobs from cheap Czech labour.

Urged on by shouts of 'Home to the Reich' and 'Through racial purity to German unity', Schönerer called for a German Empire which would protect racial purity by law, keep Slavs and Jews in inferior positions, and outlaw democrats and socialists. Pan-German student supporters, among them the young Hitler, were the most zealous. University students had already banned the offending groups from their fraternities. The latter made the sabre duel an obligatory sign of virility, worshipped Bismarck and Treitschke, and urged that Christianity be replaced with the warrior gods of the ancient Teutons. The riots in Prague were only stopped by martial law. The Austrian parliament exploded in ethnic violence, with rhetoric accompanied by fisticuffs and smashed furniture. Thus paralysed, parliament lost political significance and was bypassed by imperial decree in vital matters until the end of the Empire. Racism destroyed liberalism. When Theodor Mommsen, the German historian, heard that the Habsburgs would allow professors to lecture in Czech at the ancient University of Prague, he proposed a distinctly non-academic solution: 'We must crack Czech skulls.'

But Schönerer could not succeed. Bismarck and later the Kaiser did not want to dilute Prussian influence or upset the other great powers by Anschluss with Austria. Schönerer's anti-Catholicism, moreover, was suicidal in a land where the German peasants were famed for their piety and relied on the Church for ideas and information. Why should the upper-class establishment opt for a dubious merger with the enemies of 1866 when they themselves were secure from any possible Czech threat? As for the socialists, they functioned in a parliament with little power and were not as yet seen as a mortal threat. In 1907 the first elections held under universal manhood suffrage brought defeat to all the candidates of the Pan-German Party, including Schönerer himself.

This did not mean the extinction of ultra-conservatism in Austria. On the contrary, the elections of 1907 marked the emergence of the first political genius of the radical right in Europe, Karl Rudolph Lueger. Lueger's ultra-conservative Christian Social Peoples' Party (CSVP) swept Pan-German constituencies, added to them, and

34 Prompted by current anti-Semitic persecution, Karl Lueger as mayor of Vienna attempts to raise a new municipal loan from the Jews. Caricature from *Figaro*, 1897.

became one of the two largest political parties in Austria. The second largest was that of the Marxist Social Democrats. The voters of the Empire were more polarized into radical right and radical left than the citizens of any other European nation.

Karl Lueger was the son of a building superintendent. A lawyer, then a member of the City Council of Vienna, Lueger was elected to the Austrian parliament in 1885 and became mayor of Vienna in 1897. With each extension of universal suffrage his CSVP increased its representation. By 1907 it controlled Vienna, most provincial capitals and numerous towns. Lueger's Catholicism helped bring him success. The Church in Austria was not only the most reactionary in Europe, but it also exercised an unparalleled grip on its aristocratic, peasant and lower middle-class followers through its monopoly over education. Lueger and the Church both encouraged one of the most anti-Semitic publics west of Russia. Some of the most eminent Austrian clerics denounced Jews from the pulpit. A large proportion of the Austrian lower classes (and not a few learned scholars) really believed that Jews murdered Christian children as part of the Passover ritual. An Austrian priest, Father Sebastian Brunner, was one of the founders of modern anti-Semitism. Lueger's party members and officials regularly instructed the police to take special precautions at Passover, and introduced a variety of legislative proposals to outlaw marriages between Christians and Jews.

Lueger's Catholic rightism encompassed far more than simply anti-Semitism. He based his policies on the writings of the Popes and a variety of Catholic intellectuals. Among them were the well-known Bishop Ketteler of Mainz and the Austrian landowner, Baron von Vogelsang, who had also been the mentor of La Tour of the Action Française. In his influential Catholic journal, *Das Vaterland*, Baron Vogelsang insisted that Catholics must reject democratic liberalism because it denied the divinity of established authority and, therefore, inevitably led to anarchy and class struggle. Vogelsang expressed the same hopes for a corporate state that we have already seen in the ideas of La Tour and the Action Française. Vogelsang and Lueger both decried the influence of the 'parasites' of international finance and the big retailers who drove the small shopkeeper to the wall. Indeed, as mayor of Vienna, Lueger passed social legislation, including controls on public utilities, which protected the ordinary citizen and small proprietor. As for the socialist-voting proletariat, Vogelsang declared that 'gin and the Jewish press' had destroyed their memory of a 'truly Christian past'. Without evidence, Lueger accused the Jews of corrupting the masses by pornography and prostitution. What was this vaunted Jewish intellect, he declaimed, except shrewdness caused by lack of conscience? Was it any wonder that Jews found it so easy to manipulate and exploit the honest Christian artisan, tradesman or peasant?

At the turn of the century, Vienna was the centre of the most violent anti-Semitism in Europe. It was during the years of Lueger's rise to power that the orthodox Jews of eastern Europe streamed into the city. As we have noted, their strange appearance, religious garb and orthodox customs singled them out from the middle-class, partly assimilated and long-established Jewish communities of Vienna and western Europe. The newcomers generated more antagonism in Vienna than elsewhere both because of Catholic domination there, and because, as artisans and shopkeepers, they competed directly with lower middle-class German Catholics in an economy already bedevilled by constant crisis. The important part played by Jews in the higher levels of trade and commerce also helped to make anti-Semitism the norm among upper-class Austrians. Austrian pre-revolutionary legislation against the Jews had lasted longer than

35–36 Jewish life in Vienna, 1915. Above, Jewish second-hand clothes seller on the Naschmarkt. Below, Oriental Jews at Mathilda Square (now the Gaussplatz).

elsewhere in Europe, ending only with the brief liberalization of the 1860s. This, and the unbelievably virulent anti-Semitism of the German Austrians, drove politically conscious Jews to Zionism or the left, while those professions open to Jews – journalism, law, medicine and higher education – tended to promote liberal attitudes and thus reinforce conservative fears.*

In 1873 the most severe economic crash of the century occurred in Austria. Tens of thousands went bankrupt. Anti-Semitism swept the country, even though subsequent revelations showed extensive corruption among Catholic as well as Jewish politicians, businessmen and liberals. Lueger preferred to concentrate on Jewish involvement, as had French conservatives during public scandals. To focus antagonism on the Jews was a convenient way of removing blame from the economic system and undercutting socialist attacks on capitalism. Thus the right ignored the fate of those thousands of Jewish artisans and small tradesmen who had themselves been wiped out. Had not the Rothschilds, Lueger ranted, escaped unscathed? The terrible economic slump of the 1890s brought riots to Vienna and more votes to the CSVP. When Franz Josef, who was himself an anti-Semite, took measures to protect Jewish lives and businesses so that the economy would not suffer from Jewish emigration, the Mayor of Vienna labelled him the *Judenkaiser*.

The German peasants and artisans of rural Austria strongly supported Lueger's CSVP. Tied to the ways of their ancestors by daily routines, deeply loyal to a primitive form of Catholicism, the Austrian country-folk had far fewer contacts with the modern world than their French or German equivalents. Such contacts as did exist generated hostility. Business entrepreneurs with their cheap machine-made products threatened the markets of already hard-pressed artisans. Many peasants felt strongly the terrible injustice of working from dawn to dusk only to have their land mortgaged and themselves personally indebted to urban lawyers, bankers or money-lenders. For

---

* It is not surprising that Vienna at the turn of the century should have been the home of both Adolf Hitler and Theodor Herzl, the founder of Zionism. Herzl had once hoped to lead prominent Viennese Jews in a mass conversion to Christianity as a prelude to assimilation. Pogroms, Dreyfus, Schönerer, Lueger, the dramatic rise of the CSVP; all this helped to change his mind. Jews would have to find a home outside Europe. Herzl's *Der Judenstaat* was published in 1896. With each rise in CSVP votes those Jews who did not feel protected by wealth or high status moved to join his cause.

most rural Austrians, the parish priest was still the main source of ideas and values. Literate villagers read the extremely popular *Volksliteratur* of Adolf Pichler and Ferdinand Saar, whose tragic tales portrayed old customs now fading, a lush countryside now polluted, and embattled peasants and artisans facing economic disaster. City life was conveyed in images of moral decadence. It is not surprising that those artisans and peasants who found their skills obsolescent, or who were forced to sell ancestral plots of land and compete for unskilled jobs in the towns, flocked to Lueger's support. They murmured threateningly when Lueger informed them that the Marxist Social Democrats were led by a Jew, Viktor Adler, who, like Karl Marx, had nothing but contempt for a life of 'rural idiocy', spoke only of the needs of the proletariat and predicted that the peasant smallholder would be driven to the wall by large-scale capitalist farming.

But Lueger could not transform his parliamentary base into direct political power. As we have noted, ethnic conflicts undermined parliament, and the further polarization into left and right kept the reins of power in the hands of the traditional élites of court, bureaucracy and army. Indeed, Franz Josef had ignored Lueger's election victories four times and refused to appoint him mayor of Vienna, although he finally gave in. The Austrian aristocracy wanted nothing to do with commoners, even those who supported their values and interests. Protected from modern ideas by their Jesuit tutors, living off the income of vast estates which they did not manage themselves, even as they drifted towards suicide they remained devoted to their traditional activities: the hunt for mistress and game, gambling, the intricate snobberies of court etiquette and, perhaps appropriately, the turn-of-the-century fad for snail-racing.

Unlike Schönerer, Lueger learned to modify his attacks on the establishment. He directed his lower middle-class following to relieve their frustrations exclusively at the expense of socialists, Jews and international financiers. Increasingly, Lueger received support from high officials, including the prestigious Princes Alfred and Alois Liechtenstein. In the main, however, Lueger's stern authoritarian programme for the ruthless Germanization of the Empire and the permanent suppression of socialists and Jews seemed useful rhetoric but not necessary policy to the bulk of Austria's traditionalist élites. Naturally unwilling to follow left-wing proposals for a federated commonwealth of equal peoples, the worthies of the Empire falsely assumed that they could always handle the Slav menace by manipulating ethnic rivalries or, at the worst, by short military campaigns of repression. It really made little difference. Nothing could save the Habsburgs and their élites, and Lueger's policies would merely have brought them more swiftly to their bloody end. Continued Austrian imperialism in the east depended upon Schönerer's Pan-German policy of Anschluss.

Historians of the Nazi movement have too often neglected the crucial experience of Hitler's early years in Austria. Born in 1889, Hitler spent his childhood, youth and early manhood in Linz and Vienna. He was the son of an Austro-German lesser civil servant. Hitler was raised and schooled within a few miles of the Bohemian border, the home of the dreaded Czechs. If we are to believe his own account in *Mein Kampf*, Hitler was a Pan-German along with the bulk of his schoolmates in the *Realschule*. He reports that he was inspired by his favourite teacher, a historian of Pan-German views. Later, his arrival in Vienna coincided with Lueger's first decisive electoral victory in 1907. Schönerer and Lueger found some of their most zealous followers from among German youth moving from rural Austria to Vienna in search of work.

By the time he was 18, Hitler was already a Nazi in all important aspects, and he had found in Schönerer and Lueger his two political heroes. Schönerer's ideology was closest to that which Hitler would adopt; but from Lueger Hitler glimpsed the political and oratorical techniques by which a leader might generate powerful mass support. Already from his Austrian years, Hitler had formed his ambition to protect the superior and embattled German race against the mortal threats of Slav, Jew, democrat and socialist. Hitler's views were in no sense original or psychologically abnormal; they were simply an amalgam of the popular commonplaces of Austro-Pan-Germans. Hitler was outstanding only for his political genius.

In 1914, when Austria decided to crush Serbia, Hitler and millions of his fellow Austro-Germans ecstatically greeted the long-awaited settling of accounts between German and Slav. True to Pan-Germanism, however, Hitler dropped his allegiance to the vacillating traditionalism of the Habsburgs. He left Vienna for Germany, where he promptly volunteered to fight for the powerful and authoritarian Reich of the Hohenzollerns. Schönerer would not live to see it, but Hitler would bring Anschluss, rescue the Sudeten Germans from the

Czechs, destroy all independent Slav states in the former Austrian zone and, in 1941, strike at Russia itself – the very heart of Bolshevism and Pan-Slavism.

The First World War was instigated by the Habsburg attempt, supported by traditionalists and revolutionary conservatives alike, to end once and for all the drive of the Slavic peoples in the Empire for national autonomy. The ruling party at the court of Franz Josef hoped to humiliate the independent Kingdom of Serbia by force of arms so that it would cease its efforts to liberate and annex those Serbs still living in the Austro-Hungarian Empire. The assassination of the Archduke Franz Ferdinand was the pretext for Austrian intervention. Historians no longer dwell on the guilt of this or that nation when discussing the origins of the war of 1914–18, for no national leader was aware that the days of short and limited wars had passed, or that brinkmanship would result in the slaughter of ten millions and the destruction of the traditional European order.

Those national leaders most willing to fight were the élites of the most conservative nations – Austria, Russia and Germany. The foreign policies of the latter were dominated, not by elected representatives, but by aristocrats who, in an overwhelming majority, manned the foreign offices, embassies and general staffs of Emperor, Tsar and Kaiser. War was the vocation of noblemen, and to traditionalists war was and always had been not only the necessary means for the final resolution of international disputes, but also a moral act in its own right. Why should the masses and especially democratic and socialist pacifists have any voice in what, in any event, would be the sacrifices of professional armies? The vast majority of the decision-makers in 1914 assumed that, as in the past, the conflict would last for only a few months, and would be decided by cavalry charges, swift advances on major cities and brief pitched battles by professional armies fighting with previously stocked reserves of ammunition. There would, the old leaders assumed, be little civilian involvement. Only a few military experts foresaw that industrial technology had revolutionized warfare by making the defensive far superior to the offensive. The machine-gun, rapid-fire artillery and the new-found ability to move reserves by railway to threatened salients brought stalemate in the west. Civilians turned soldiers were thus condemned to futile slaughter in vain assaults against well-prepared trenchworks.

Most crucial of all, the dispute which had been started by the two most backward powers, Austria and Russia, could only be settled by the more advanced nations of the West. The Austrian and Russian élites were not able to survive, let alone win, a war which could only be fought to advantage by nations which possessed a vast industrial capacity; a capacity which required both a large industrial-based proletariat to produce the means of war, and a skilled middle class to organize the restructuring of the economy. The two multi-national Empires also lacked the other major requirement for total war: a loyal body of citizens who would identify their fate with that of their governments under even the most trying circumstances. By 1916 millions of ill-equipped Russian peasant-soldiers were being slain by German bullets and explosives. By 1917 vast numbers had deserted to join their fellow Russians in a civil war against the remnants of tsarism. With a few notable exceptions, the ethnic minorities of Austria-Hungary were only willing to defend their own territories, and were otherwise either apathetic or downright hostile. By 1917 Austria's armies were extremely unreliable. Loyal troops shot thousands of deserters and 'traitors', including on occasion the inhabitants of whole villages. Some minority units, notably 130,000 Czechs, even fought for the Allies. Before the war ended, the Austrian Empire was falling apart.

Russia and Austria had long sought to dominate the Balkan states, especially since the collapse of the Ottoman Empire. When Russia defeated the Turks in 1875–78, the Serbs took advantage of the embarrassment of their Ottoman masters and gained an independent Kingdom of Serbia after a brief war of national liberation. At the Congress of Berlin (1878) the great powers refused to allow Russia to set up an extensive satellite system in the Balkans. As Metternich had once noted, Serbia must be either Turkish or Austrian, for then the balance of power would remain unaffected. Austria was, therefore, allowed to occupy the Turkish province of Bosnia-Herzogovina, in order to keep Russian and Serbian Pan-Slavism at bay. The Serb peasants of the province had been mercilessly brutalized by the Turks and their Muslim landlords. Austrian rule was little better, and the Serbs countered with guerrilla warfare. The conflict had results with which we have become familiar in our own century: razed villages, the killing of non-combatants, terror and counter-terror. The Serbs in Bosnia fought to join the independent Kingdom of Serbia, whose peasants were significantly better-off economically. Led by the radical nationalist, Nikola Pashich, and aided by Russia, Serbia hoped to gain some 4 million compatriots from Austro-Hungarian rule.

Franz Josef, his advisers, and Conrad, his Chief of Staff, were well aware that Serbian success would mean the ultimate dismemberment of the Empire and Russian domination of the Balkans. Austrian ruling circles urged the Emperor to move to a final confrontation with Serbia. In 1912–13 Serbia and other Balkan nations combined to drive Turkey from her remaining European possessions. In the process, Serbia conquered territories which would give her an outlet to the sea and further power to unite all southern Slavs. In October 1913 Austria's Foreign Minister, Count Berchtold, issued an ultimatum to Serbia: surrender the conquered territories within a week or face war. The German Emperor informed the Serbs that they must obey the will of Franz Josef, or Belgrade would be bombarded and the German sword unsheathed. Serbia and Russia backed down. Nevertheless, all sections of the right in Austria were furious with Berchtold for not simply invading Serbia without hesitation. Austria's ruling élites were also extremely fearful of the coming reign of the heir to the throne, the Archduke Franz Ferdinand. He was known to favour concessions to the southern Slavs. The pro-war faction at court heaved a sigh of relief when the Archduke was assassinated by pro-Serb terrorists in Sarajevo, the capital of Bosnia, on 28 June 1914. Although at the time there was no evidence of Serbian involvement in the assassination, the Serbs could now be crushed on the pretext of righteous moral outrage.

In Germany the Kaiser, along with most of his military leaders and aristocratic advisers, was anxious to support and encourage Austria in her conflict with Serbia and Russia. German 'global' policy demanded the domination of eastern and south-eastern Europe. Germany now led Europe in iron and steel output, population growth and military expenditure, and was second in coal production. As the Chief of the General Staff, von Moltke, had warned more than once, Russian industrialization and railway construction, crucial for the mobilization of army reserves, were proceeding apace. Moreover, German conservatives needed an aggressive foreign policy to bolster their weakening hold on Germany's future. Their old rural constituencies were being eroded by industrialization, urbanization and social mobility; the middle classes were gaining power at their expense; and the electoral power of the socialists increased alarmingly with each year. The Kaiser, with customary frankness, put it simply: if war comes the socialists must be eliminated, by a bloodbath if necessary. Meanwhile the nation must be psychologically prepared for the life-and-death struggle against the Slavs.

This could have been dismissed as empty bombast had not the constitution given full powers over war and peace to the Kaiser, who relied for advice on like-minded military chiefs and was able to ignore opposition views. Bethmann-Hollweg, Imperial Chancellor from 1909 to 1917, had no independent power base among Germany's political parties, and was, therefore, totally dependent on extra-parliamentary and conservative élites. Large sections of German middle-class opinion also supported an aggressive foreign policy, as was shown by the enormous popularity of General von Bernhardi's *Germany and the Next War* of which there were four editions in 1912 alone. Bernhardi called for German domination as far as the borders of Russia, military action to prevent French interference, and an aggressive campaign of overseas imperialism.

Thus, with only occasional doubts, the German government gave Austria full support; indeed, it egged on the hesitant Austrian court. This was the logical culmination of Treitschke's projection of the policy of 'blood and iron' beyond unification. Certain of German support should Russia aid Serbia, the Austrian government issued its famous ultimatum on 23 July. Some of its terms were designed to be unacceptable to any independent nation; all terms were to be accepted in 48 hours. Following Russian advice, Serbia arranged to appear as the innocent victim by accepting almost all the demands on 25 July. To Moltke's delight, the Russian government gave orders to prepare for mobilization. Austria rejected the Serb reply with contempt and declared war against Serbia at 11 a.m. on 28 July. The Tsar ordered partial mobilization of his troops on the same day, while Russia's ally France gave assurances of full support. The British urged negotiations. In response, the Kaiser and Bethmann-Hollweg took the high-minded but transparent position that the conflict ought to be limited to Austria and Serbia. This meant that Austria would be able to conquer Serbia without Russian interference.

Russia could hardly back down again. A diplomatic setback of such magnitude would not merely end Russian influence in the Balkans. Continued German pressure and victories might lead to revolution at home, or even to the breakaway of some of the less 'russified' ethnic groups bordering on the west. The German General Staff was aware that Russia must fight, and that France was not likely to sit idly by and watch Germany become a global power. Thus the famous Schlieffen plan of the German army. France was to be invaded immediately through Belgium and Luxemburg, while Austrian and some German troops would hold back the Russians until, France defeated, German troops could be moved in force to challenge the slowly mobilizing giant in the east. If, as expected, France were to fall within a few weeks, Great Britain would not be able to send sufficient troops to change the outcome.

Since 1906, the German army had made the two-front war always feared by Bismarck a matter of policy because only thus could German dominance in the east be assured. On 30 July Russia's military leaders finally persuaded a frightened Tsar to mobilize against Germany as well as Austria. This was enough for the real leaders of Germany, the military. Even as Bethmann-Hollweg asked Berchtold of Austria to keep negotiating with Russia on 30 July, Count von Moltke telephoned his Austrian military counterpart, Conrad, and urged him to mobilize against Russia. On 31 July this was done. Bismarck had always kept his generals in check; but the legacy of his policies had been to give the military free rein to pre-empt diplomatic negotiations. On 31 July Germany issued the decisive ultimata. Russia must suspend mobilization within twelve hours; France must promise to remain neutral and show good faith by the immediate surrender of the fortresses of Toul and Verdun. Not surprisingly, Russia and France turned down Germany's offer to surrender without a fight. On 1 August Germany declared war on Russia and invaded Luxemburg. On 2 August von Moltke demanded that Belgium allow German troops to occupy her territory until the end of the war. Belgium refused and was invaded on 3 August; on the same day Germany declared war on France. Great Britain demanded that Germany pull her troops out of Belgium. When the Germans refused, Great Britain declared war on 4 August.

The German Foreign Office professed surprise at Great Britain's response, but in diplomatic circles it had long been common knowledge that Great Britain would never allow the Channel ports to fall to any great power. Bethmann-Hollweg revealed some talent for the theatre when he feigned shock before the Reichstag at this alleged act of British perfidy. He also demonstrated the usual conservative contempt for elected representatives of the people by his claim that Germany's acts over the past weeks had been dictated solely by the law of self-preservation.

Shocked by the terrible savagery of 1914–18, historians have looked for commensurate guilt or profound explanations. But the war was the result of the accepted system of international confrontation developed in the pre-industrial era of great-power politics; confrontations carried on for limited aims and by means of limited war. No nation was guilty of a crime. Wars were not then defined as crimes, and none of the decision-makers foresaw the terrors of total war. No peoples were responsible because the decisions were made by a handful of leaders. Those leaders who did most to initiate the conflict were acting in response to traditional conservative policies. Austria's attempt to crush Serbia and preserve her own decaying Empire was the last chapter in a struggle extending back to the time of Metternich. Russia's response to Austria and her support of Serbia was also an attempt to bolster the reactionary social order of tsarist autocracy. It was typical of Russian and Austrian ultra-conservatism that few who had any voice at all foresaw that victory and even survival would only go to those nations able to harness the dynamic forces of industrialism and nationalism.

In the end, it was German intervention which escalated a conflict between pre-modern traditionalists into a war between advanced industrial nations with skilled and loyal populations. The dynamic new right wing of Germany responded with reflexes originally conditioned and given high status by Bismarck's policy of 'blood and iron'. Success in war would dampen domestic discontent, re-establish the prestige and values of rightist élites and curb the threatening rise of democratic liberalism and socialism. Moving beyond mere unification, the leaders of the Reich could clear the way for permanent German dominance throughout central and eastern Europe. Germany would rank with the United States and Great Britain as a *Weltmacht*. With this vision, the new right united with the old and dragged Europe over the brink.

IX CONSERVATISM AND THE RADICAL RIGHT AFTER 1918

The trauma of tens of millions of deaths and mutilations in the First World War affected nearly every family in Europe and radically transformed European society and politics for a generation and more. It was no longer possible to view the steady progress of Western civilization with any complacency; indeed, to many the latter now seemed suicidal by its very nature. Revolutionary rejections of past norms became general in all areas of society and culture. In ideology and politics, the extremes of both right and left gained at the expense of the middle parties, whose members continued to function as though the old system still prevailed or could be restored. The values and practices of liberalism had suffered immensely in the drive towards total war. On the Continent civil rights and parliamentary rule were suppressed in favour of *de facto* military dictatorship. *Laissez-faire* was abandoned as too inefficient when survival was at stake; economies were planned, labour forces mobilized and directed, and vast armies were forged from civilian populations. Censorship and government-sponsored propaganda generated a mindless ultra-patriotism. This and the deep anger caused by seemingly endless casualties helped to create a hatred for the 'enemy' among the civilian public who otherwise would have had to face the terrible fact that their sons, fathers, husbands and brothers had all died in vain. The slaughter of the war far outweighed the importance of the goals for which any nation had fought.

The ranks of the aristocracy of Europe had been drastically reduced by the savage slaughter of their officer sons at the front. The middle classes saw an abrupt end to their steady progress and were battered by post-war inflation. The proletariat saw the gains which they had made during the pre-war decades wiped out. The peasantry, who had supplied most of the men and the casualties at the front, found themselves plunged into an immediate post-war rural depression as the war-stimulated markets for their goods melted away. Perhaps the most bitter of all were the survivors of the trenches. Often expecting rewards for their sacrifices, they were greeted by social chaos, inflation and unemployment.

37 Demonstration of German war veterans. Design by Fritz Arnold for
Simplicissimus, from the series 'The war as I saw it', 1918.

Though it is true that many ex-soldiers of lower rank supported the left, the large and official veterans' organizations, dominated by ex-officers, were ultra-rightist and often provided the nuclei for the bewildering variety of semi-fascist organizations which emerged in the post-war years. As for the rest of society, excluding the very well-off, within a decade the Great Depression was to destroy what little stability remained.

Paradoxically, the success of Bolshevism in Russia and elsewhere at the end of the war favoured conservatives in the advanced industrial nations over the long run. Most of the population of western Europe had some stake, however minimal, in established institutions, governments, property and status. When threatened from the left, the bulk of the population moved to the right to protect that stake, especially in times of economic chaos. The prominence of left-wing intellectuals has promoted the myth that it was the left who made the greatest advances during the inter-war years. However, aided by the shocks of war, inflation and depression, the various right-wing and fascist movements gained far more in numbers and political power. Advanced industrial nations seemed to offer little potential for radical left-wing revolutions. As we shall see, the same could not be said of revolutions from the radical right.

38   'Do you want this?' Anti-Bolshevik poster by Paul Helwig, 1919.

In November 1919 French conservatives won their greatest electoral victory since 1871. The Chamber was once again thick with ex-military officers and practising Catholics. But the policies followed by conservative governments during the inter-war years were not those of the royalist or radical right. Governments tended to act in the spirit of the bourgeois conservatism associated with men like Clemenceau and Poincaré. Property rights came first. Close attention was paid to the interests of the larger economic interests of France. The wealthy were to be lightly taxed. Social-welfare legislation would be avoided. Ultra-nationalism would be stressed. Above all, the 'red menace' must be crushed. When faced with economic crises, conservative governments followed policies which favoured the powerful and propertied. The salaries of lesser public officials were cut, taxes were lowered and public spending, especially for social welfare, was cut to the bone. To protect the franc and to avoid taxing the wealthy, conservative governments preferred, paradoxically, to borrow rather than pay costs as they arose. Thus short-term bonds were sold to a minority of extreme wealth. This meant that governments daring to risk 'New Deal' policies of social reform could be and often were brought down by the threat of the financial community to pull its money out of government bonds. In the case of worker unrest, as in 1919, conservative governments were prone to use police, troops and eager strike-breakers from the patriotic leagues rather than yield.

Foreign policy was also a means to defend the *status quo*. Vast German reparations would enable the government to keep taxes low and still repair the damage done to France by a war largely carried out on her soil. Moreover, statistics showed that France would be permanently weaker than Germany in terms of population growth and industrial production unless a harsh peace treaty kept Germany inferior. Some voices from the left indicated that Germany was now ruled by republicans and socialists, not the Kaiser and his generals, so that harsh terms might only revive the militant nationalism of the German right by focusing discontent upon the left. This was correct, but bitter outrage at the horror of the war left no popular support for pacification. Germany should be dismembered, her industry dismantled, her material resources seized, her treasure taken and her army kept at the level of a police force. Had the Germans won, they would undoubtedly have demanded at least as much, as witness the Treaty of Brest-Litovsk.

The Allies forced Clemenceau to settle for much less than his maximum demands, with the result that his own public called him a traitor while British and American leaders – protected by Channel and ocean – accused him of excessive harshness. France did gain reparations, the right to exploit the Saar coalfields for fifteen years, a demilitarized Rhineland, extensive material resources and a German army reduced to 100,000 men. In 1923, however, the German government demonstrated the impossibility of keeping a potentially more powerful nation permanently weak by French action alone. On the pretext of German non-cooperation with the terms of the Versailles Treaty, Poincaré employed the usual military 'solution' and invaded the Ruhr. Allied antagonism and German passive resistance forced a withdrawal. Only the various demagogues of the radical right gained, for the French had effectively demonstrated the need for a German military revival (this was the year of Hitler's Munich *Putsch*). Regardless of the moral complexities involved in the Versailles settlements, no German government could long obey terms rejected by 90 per cent of its people, and France did not have the power to occupy Germany permanently. In short, French conservative foreign policy merely fed the German ultra-nationalist right.

The Great Depression brought a revival of the radical right in France and in Europe generally. The Depression came late to France and did not create the massive unemployment suffered in Germany. But French industry recovered at a slower rate than that of any advanced nation. This was partly because conservative governments worsened matters by refusing to stimulate purchasing power through public spending. Instead, budgets were cut at the expense of the salaries of civil servants and those few social services that did exist. The multi-party political system of France could protect a variety of private economic interests, but it could not unite behind a programme to resolve the crisis for the community as a whole. Economic stagnation, political paralysis and government scandals were compounded by the failure of conservative foreign policy. In 1932 Chancellor Brüning of Germany refused to pay any more reparations. Sentiment against the Third Republic increased on both left and right. When the government dismissed the right-wing head of the police, ultra-conservative patriotic leagues, including members of the Action Française, took to the streets in massive riots. This has often been seen mistakenly as a close brush with fascism. In reality, there could be no successful *coup* or 'march on Rome', for the police and the army remained loyal to the Republic. Neither the bulk of the voters nor the governing élites saw the need to do more than form a new 'government of national union' of the same bourgeois conservative type that had ruled almost without break since the war.

The riots were a sign of the revival of the radical right, however, and this in turn gave new unity to the left. Radicals who feared for the Republic, and Communists who finally perceived the dangers of fascism, united behind the leadership of Léon Blum, who in 1936 became the first socialist premier of France. Blum hoped to increase the salaries of public employees and workers' wages, and to use public spending in ways that would increase sales, investment, employment and general well-being. But, though united in defence of the Republic, his unstable coalition could not resolve the paradoxes of governing a nation polarized between left and right. From the start the Communists refused to participate. When Blum, lacking British support, refused to risk civil war in France by open intervention against Franco in Spain, the Communists reverted to the old Stalinist tactic of labelling socialists as fascist stooges.

Nor was Blum helped by the massive sit-down strikes which occurred when he gained office, strikes led by workers hoping for immediate benefits. French capitalists, momentarily forgetting their ultra-patriotism, increased the economic chaos by sending their capital to safe havens abroad. Finally, Blum was warned by the financial community that they would aid the government only if he dropped his social legislation and cut government expenditure. Thus emasculated, Blum's policies could not stimulate industrial recovery. In fact, the costs of his social legislation diverted some capital from investment, while the salary and wage increases gained by his Popular Front were spent mostly on food – a comment on the living standards of the lower classes.

In June 1937 French capitalists provided the *coup de grâce* by refusing to purchase government bonds. Blum could remain premier only if he allowed his policies to be dictated by the upper middle classes. He resigned. Thus the moderate conservatives of France proved that they could control events without the services of a French Hitler.

Nevertheless, in the late 1930s a wealth of ultra-right and fascist groups flourished briefly in France, often taking Mussolini as their model. All were a response to the stagnation of the economy during the Depression years, the threat posed by the increasing popularity of socialism and communism, and the initial successes of the Popular Front led by one who was both a socialist and a Jew. Besides the still influential Action Française, the most important of the many groups were Colonel de la Rocque's Croix de Feu, Jacques Doriot's Parti Populaire Français, Georges Valois's Faisceau, François Coty's Solidarité Française, Marcel Bucard's Francistes, Pierre Taittinger's Jeunesse Patriotes, the terrorist Cagoulards ('hooded ones') and Henri Dorgère's Défense Paysanne, whose 'green shirts' attracted perhaps half a million peasants. These groups, and others like them, were para-military and authoritarian; all hoped for a strong leader to repress the Republic through *coup* or revolution. Each expressed with variations ideals roughly similar to those of the Action Française and Mussolini's Fascists: the warrior ethic, ultra-nationalism, the cult of virility, ruralism, patriarchy, imperialism and anti-communism. Their supporters tended to come from the same classes and groups which supported the Action Française and European fascism in general.

Fascism itself failed in France because it could not put together the combination which brought Mussolini and Hitler to power. In nations with weak republican traditions, the radical right became necessary to traditional conservatives who were threatened from the left, had lost their customary followings and needed right-wing social movements capable of gathering masses of lower-class votes. Few voters were attracted to French fascism, for the government was not hard-pressed to defend private property. Although French fascists had many wealthy supporters and admirers among the traditional conservative élites, few felt desperate enough to reach out for the demagogues of the right. The moderate conservative rulers of France never lost their large share of the electorate. Furthermore, they had brought down the Popular Front with ease. The Depression had been relatively moderate. Two generations of Frenchmen had been educated in a republican environment. The Republic had won the war and the army was content. Alsace-Lorraine and a larger empire had been gained. France had no further demands to make apart from that of keeping Germany weak. In addition, clergy, military and middle class alike were gratified that Blum had not dared, as the

Archbishop of Paris put it, to aid Soviet atheism against Franco, the representative of Christian civilization.

After 1935, however, the French right found it more difficult to maintain a popular and consistent attitude towards foreign policy. It was easy to be against the Weimar Republic because intense antagonism against the Germans coincided with contempt for republican institutions. When Hitler gained power, the French radical right could still disguise its affinity for Nazi ideology and emphasize instead its admiration for Mussolini. When Mussolini invaded Ethiopia, it became less easy to be simultaneously anti-German and pro-Fascist, because French-supported sanctions against Italy helped put Mussolini in the German camp. A furious Maurras called for the assassination of Blum and those deputies who had supported Ethiopia; for this he spent a few months in jail.

After 1935 the French right moved increasingly towards appeasement, even as the left took a strong anti-fascist line. Indeed, with the victory of the Popular Front many an upper-class dining-room resounded with the slogan 'Better Hitler than Blum'. Jacques Bainville, along with Maurras one of the 'forty immortals' of the French Academy, spoke for many when he insisted that France had no quarrel with the Germans and ought to help them crush Bolshevism and build a new European order. Most liberal leaders, fearful of another 1914–18, greeted the Munich settlement with a sigh of relief. The French right went beyond this and thought it a matter of simple justice that the Czechs should yield the Sudetenland to Hitler. The left insisted that only force would stop Hitler. The French right and centre continued to hope that appropriate compromises would satisfy him. Unexpected allies joined the right when the Nazi-Soviet Non-Aggression Pact was signed in August 1939. European communists suddenly discovered that the true enemies of the workers were not the Nazis but Polish landlords and British and French imperialists, as A. J. P. Taylor has noted.

When the invasion of Poland brought Great Britain and a reluctant France into the war, Maurras remained true to his past beliefs. France should surrender. Why fight Hitler merely to aid Bolsheviks and Jews and prepare the way for a left-wing revolution in France itself? Let Hitler crush the Bolsheviks, Maurras insisted; France must be kept neutral and strong. During the Vichy régime Maurras's voice would be heard to more decisive effect.

France's defeat brought the hero of Verdun, Marshal Pétain, to power in unoccupied or Vichy France. The régime was not fascist though the ultra-right participated heavily. As Robert Paxton has indicated in his definitive work, *Vichy France*, the régime was the 'last stand' of those traditional conservatives who for decades had opposed the coming of modernism in all its forms. Its supporters were the usual groups: royalists, including the pretender, the bulk of the Church and military hierarchies, and a high proportion of businessmen and small property-owners who had recently moved to the right as a response to the rise of the left. (By 1936 the Socialist Party had become the largest in France, and the Communists received 20 per cent of the total vote.)

The actions of Vichy France were limited by time and the Germans. More than the leaders of any other occupied country, however, Pétain and his associates were willing to cooperate with the Germans. Their voluntary collaboration shows how traditional conservatives tended, in times of crisis, to blur ideological distinctions between themselves and the radical revolutionaries to their right. Pétain, Laval and their supporters hoped to become equal partners in Hitler's Europe. German troops were granted the use of French imperial territories and bases, and Vichy leaders offered to join the war against the Allies on an equal basis. Nazi distrust and Hitler's contempt, not Vichy reluctance, kept them from partnership in the Thousand Year Reich.

Pétain had been voted full power by the majority of deputies. There were many reasons for this, but conservatives were powerfully motivated by the conviction that authoritarian leadership was an appropriate response to defeat. After all, had not France been rendered easy prey for Teutonic discipline by over two generations of republican individualism, materialism, secularism, democracy and socialist internationalism? (Maurras, for one, welcomed the death of French democracy even if by force of German arms.) Despite conservative arguments, France actually lost because her ageing (and conservative) generals had remained wedded to the static defensive strategy which had enabled them to survive the First World War. They were content to crouch behind the Maginot Line – the ultimate trenchwork – or hold fixed positions to its north and await the

German frontal assault. But tanks, aircraft and motorized infantry columns had made lightning offensive thrusts once again a decisive factor in battle, as many of the younger officers of Europe, including the then Colonel de Gaulle, were well aware. In any event, even those Frenchmen who had no ideological reason for supporting Pétain could not envisage any alternative. Until the tide of battle turned against the Germans in 1943, England, despite Churchill's rhetoric, could do little, and Russia seemed on the verge of defeat.

Pétain once called Maurras the most French of Frenchmen, and it was the ideology of the Action Française combined with older conservative notions that permeated Pétain's hopes for a new France. Maurras himself played no active role in Vichy. He was content to publish the names of anti-Nazi Frenchmen so as to see them jailed, tortured or shot. Vichy leaders themselves purged and punished large numbers of liberals, socialists, communists, Jews and Freemasons (the latter had been among the most zealous defenders of liberalism, and had also aided republican leaders in their purge of conservative office-holders in the immediate aftermath of the Dreyfus affair). Within limits set by the Germans, the basic policy decisions during Vichy were made by the following groups: notables of wealth and high position, senior civil servants, graduates of the select schools which had traditionally trained conservative élites, and the heads of corporate business. Local officials, once elected, were now appointed from above. French fascists, too extreme and unpredictable for Pétain and his traditionalists, were kept out of policy-making positions but were used widely as leaders of youth groups, in propaganda posts and in repressive police and para-military units.

Pétain abolished republican institutions and wanted to replace them with corporate groups representing regions, trades, vocations and professions. These would advise the head of state who would retain final power. However, little was done to carry out this hallowed piece of conservative political theory. Vichy did have the time and will to restore some former Church properties, favour parochial education and permit religious orders to teach once again. Radicals, republicans and Jews were dismissed from the teaching profession. (The National Teachers' Union had been strongly anti-fascist.) For the revolutionary slogan of liberty, equality and fraternity, Vichy substituted a new national rallying-cry: work, family, fatherland.

Under Vichy, workers were denied the right to strike. As in Stalin's Russia, trade unions functioned to locate, deflect and suppress worker discontent. In spite of the writings of La Tour, Leo XIII and a generation of Social Catholics, the Christian conscience of the owners and managers of business under Vichy did not prevent the industrial proletariat from suffering the largest decline in real income of any social class. As in Mussolini's corporate state, rhetoric disguised the simple truth that businessmen were allowed to regulate themselves and in accord with their own interests. Of course, in France they were subject to the heavy demands of the German war machine, but this also was not unprofitable.

Predictably, Vichy introduced legislation to aid the artisans and craftsmen of France as well as the peasantry. More than any other class, the sturdy Catholic peasant had been idealized by French conservatives. Was he not the living symbol of ancestral traditions and the embodiment, therefore, of what G. K. Chesterton once called the 'democracy of the dead'? Besieged by rural interests for economic protection, Vichy leaders made efforts to aid the small family farm. But German demands for foodstuffs, the requirements of economic rationalization and the influence of wealthy and powerful landed interests proved more powerful than the populist nostalgia of traditionalists. As Paxton aptly puts it, in all areas of French society Vichy 'spoiled' the rich. Beyond temporarily emasculating the workers and the left, the Vichy régime made no lasting structural changes in French society.

Even without the German occupation it is doubtful whether those seriously committed to restoring pre-revolutionary attitudes and institutions could ever have avoided functioning as the tools of the less ideologically motivated and more economically powerful and entrenched upper-class élites. The results of economic modernization could hardly be reversed, even if liberal-democratic political institutions could be suppressed.

Thus the Vichy régime was restricted to mounting an intensive campaign intended to reverse the decay of traditional values and halt what one leading French fascist intellectual called the 'progress of decadence' in Europe. The usual manifestations of moral decay and permissiveness were denounced: sexual laxity, easy divorce, revealing fashions, excessive consumption of alcohol, and the corruption and rootlessness of city life. French youth were urged to

39   Fascism French-style. Commemorative rally for the second anniversary of the
Lyons legion, 1940.

return to the Church, the land and the ethic of work. The
government, Church organizations and fascist-led youth groups
staged the elaborate para-military ceremonies common to right-wing
régimes, with their heavy use of symbols intended to awaken
nostalgia for an idealized past. The young were organized in semi-
military hiking, camping and sporting leagues. Here the virtues of a
rural life of ascetic simplicity and hard work were stressed, and the
patriarchal structure and ancient faith and customs of village life held
up as models. Pétain and Vichy propagandists emphasized above all
the need for each citizen to subordinate himself to the greater good of
France and to do so in a spirit of self-sacrificial obedience to
established authority. There was little to distinguish Vichy rhetoric
from that of Fascist Italy, and nothing to indicate any lasting impact
on public consciousness.

The anti-Semitic policies of Vichy were directed by members or
former members of the Action Française and other ultra-patriotic
right-wing leagues. For the most part Vichy's extensive anti-Semitic

activities were not the result of Nazi pressure, but the consequence of the traditional anti-Semitism of French conservatives. Pétain was himself a vigorous anti-Semite. Under his régime thousands of Jews were dismissed from political and civil service posts, and strict quotas severely limited Jewish participation in banking, finance, education and the professions. Unlike the Nazis, French officials sometimes exempted decorated war veterans or Jews of great wealth from such measures. Nevertheless, Jewish assets and property were seized, and thousands of Jews were deprived of citizenship, interned in labour camps and handed over to Himmler for extermination in Nazi death-camps.

The eager collaboration of Vichy made little difference to the Nazis. France was more exploited than any other occupied country in the west. Raw materials, foodstuffs and industrial products were requisitioned in huge quantities by the Germans. Frenchmen accounted for the largest number of foreign males engaged in forced labour in Germany. Hitler neither needed nor wished to grant any other nation partnership in his empire.

The rule of the French conservatives in Vichy was totally dependent on German victories. By 1943 Allied successes caused a

40 Detail from a travelling anti-Jewish exhibition, Paris 1941.

dramatic increase in French resistance. Typically, the Nazis responded with the mass murder of innocent hostages – even Pétain protested. But the ultra-right extremists who manned Vichy's punitive units managed to persuade the old warrior that the resistance was dominated by traitors and communists. Accordingly, Pétain permitted Darnand, the fascist head of the French militia, to select the hostages from known enemies of the régime. Thus Frenchmen ended up murdering Frenchmen for Germans.

As the Allied invasion drew nearer, the affinity between traditional and revolutionary conservatives was increasingly revealed. Pétain gloomily predicted that Bolshevik Russia and the 'Jewish' United States would now decide the fate of France and Europe. Maurras was desperate: France would suffer another 1789, he predicted, and he advised Pétain to execute all those who aided the Allies, including their families. As the Allies advanced, Pétain was taken by the Germans to one of the Hohenzollern castles, an apt symbol of the dilemma of the French right in the wake of German power. Pétain was too French to remain head of the government under such circumstances. He was replaced by the fascist Doriot until the latter was killed when an Allied plane strafed his car. Many French fascists remained loyal to their convictions until the end, and a significant number died fighting with the SS in Russia. After the war, Darnand and Laval were executed by the French; Pétain and Maurras were sentenced to life imprisonment. For Maurras it was, as he said, 'the revenge of Dreyfus'.

Even if collaboration had not discredited traditional conservatism, the Vichy experience convinced the bulk of its supporters that the ideals of the distant past could never reverse the process of modernization or be a significant political force in France. There have been brief revivals of the radical right in France since Vichy, notably when the French military was forced to return both Indochina and Algeria to their original inhabitants, but no popular echo of major political impact resulted. There is still a pretender to the throne, the present Comte de Paris, who regards himself as Henri VI, King of France. He issues a monthly bulletin on political matters to the remnants of the faithful, and maintains himself in dignified irrelevance in his manor-house outside Paris. The hopes and prospects of both traditional conservatives and the radical right were destroyed in the conflagrations of the Second World War.

X THE RADICAL RIGHT IN AUSTRIA
AND GERMANY 1918–45

Austria was driven rapidly to the right by the aftermath of the First World War and the economic chaos of the inter-war years. The political history of Austria until Hitler's invasion is one of the rule of traditional conservatives strongly supported by the radical right, with a gradual drift into what has been aptly described as a régime of 'clerical fascism'.

By 1918 all the fears of the pre-war Austro-German right had been realized. The Slav successor states had inherited the bulk of the imperial Habsburg territories. The Bolsheviks controlled Russia and, together with the newly established Communist régime in Hungary and Slav troops, were attacking areas that had once been part of the Empire. Even the lowly Serbs had emerged from the war with larger territories, now called Yugoslavia, and were still on the offensive. Austria herself was now a tiny state economically dependent on her former enemies, the Allies, whose loans were all that kept her from going bankrupt. Not surprisingly, during the 1920s every Austrian political party wanted Anschluss with Germany, but the economic leverage of the Allies and French fears of a greater Germany prevented this. Finally, Austria was swollen with impoverished German refugees who had fled or been driven from homes and jobs in the newly established successor states. These refugees would support any force that might restore the Empire and their lost status, and hence would gravitate towards the right.

Even though Austria was a democratic and socialist republic in 1920, this was only a temporary result of defeat in war and could hardly be expected to last. The bulk of the Austrian right, and for that matter the left, hoped for far more extreme and revolutionary solutions than democratic and moderate socialists could provide in such a war-torn, polarized and bankrupt state. Thus, as elsewhere in central and eastern Europe, armed right-wing and semi-fascist groups sprang up in Austria; the most important of these was the Heimwehr led by Prince Starhemberg. The members of the Heimwehr hoped to

41 The burning of the symbols of the Habsburg monarchy on the declaration of the Czechoslovak Republic, Prague 1919.

defend their fatherland from its ethnic and left-wing enemies, and perhaps one day even regain the lost imperial territories. With a new violence born of intense frustrations, Heimwehr leaders propagated ideas made familiar by Schönerer and Lueger; their ranks were swelled by displaced aristocrats, military officers, embittered refugees, and small and large property-owners frightened by Bolshevik and socialist gains. Austrian socialism was more militant and revolutionary than elsewhere in Europe and this, in turn, intensified the conservative backlash.

Nevertheless, until Hitler's invasion, and after a brief interlude of socialist rule, the traditional conservatives of the Christian Social Party held on to the chancellorship, using the Heimwehr as street-fighters against the left. But the Depression of 1929 created further extremist unrest on both left and right. The Social Democratic Party was able to gain some 40 per cent of the electorate; and tens of thousands of frightened and angry bourgeois flocked to the standards of the Heimwehr. The clerical leaders of the ruling Christian Social Party appointed Prince Starhemberg to the cabinet, while the Church placed socialists under interdict so that they were refused sacraments

42 'The day is dawning!' The 1923 Munich *Putsch* as depicted by the Nazi propagandist Mjölnir.

and could not attain a state of grace. The ruling conservatives did not wish to encourage their competitors on the right too strongly unless absolutely necessary; when Starhemberg failed to gain significant electoral successes in 1931 he was dropped from the cabinet. Infuriated at this 'betrayal' by the conservatives of the official government party, Heimwehr units attempted a *Putsch* in the same year, aided by local officials and police. But the army remained neutral, socialists took to the streets and the *Putsch* failed. Starhemberg still hoped that events would make him Austria's Mussolini. In 1931 Chancellor Dollfuss proposed a customs union with Germany in an attempt to pre-empt the issue which seemed to aid the right the most, that of Anschluss. The government was humiliated when the French forced Dollfuss to back down. Moreover, when Dollfuss was forced to ask for Allied aid to pull Austria back from the brink of certain bankruptcy, he was denied it until he forswore future attempts at unity with Germany. The result was a new surge to the right among Austrians who felt increasingly oppressed, economically and politically, by Allied hypocrisy over the issue of national self-determination.

But the Christian Social Party and the Heimwehr had powerful rivals for allegiance in Austria. The dynamic rise of Hitler in the early 1930s gave the previously weak Austrian Nazis a new political importance, especially after Hitler's decisive electoral success in 1932. Excluding the left, the Austrian public increasingly demanded Anschluss with Germany. The Christian Social Party could not and did not want to merge totally with Germany and lose its own identity. Starhemberg hoped to maintain Austrian independence so that he might fulfil his goal of becoming dictator. Both parties were blamed for the Austrian impasse, because without joining Germany there could be no economic recovery. In 1932 the Austrian Nazis received 16 per cent of the vote, and almost captured the Vienna City Council as well. After Hitler's appointment as German chancellor in 1933, Austrian Nazi votes increased rapidly, reaching as high as 40 per cent in provincial elections.

As we shall see, the traditional conservatives of Germany needed the Nazis partly because their own voting base had withered. But the Christian Social Party of Austria steadily managed to retain one-third of the electorate. Chancellor Dollfuss, therefore, did not need to conciliate the Austrian Nazis; instead, he moved his traditionalists further to the right in order to attract Nazi supporters. Dollfuss had the socialist stronghold of Vienna, the Karl Marx Hof, bombarded and captured in February 1934. Socialists were disarmed, disbanded and jailed. Dollfuss then suspended parliament, appointed Starhemberg vice-chancellor, drove the Nazis underground and proceeded to form his own clerical–fascist ruling party, the Fatherland Front. In the streets, Heimwehr fascists fought Austrian Nazis to keep them from power and to maintain Austrian independence from Germany – the one issue which separated these two major organizations of revolutionary conservatism.

In July 1934, probably with Hitler's approval, the Vienna SS of the Austrian Nazis murdered Dollfuss and attempted a *Putsch*. Not wanting a greater German Reich poised on the borders of Italy, Mussolini moved his troops to the Brenner Pass. Starhemberg rushed home from a visit to Italy, and the police put down the revolt with ease. With Mussolini's approval, Kurt von Schuschnigg became the new Führer of the Fatherland Front. Consolidating his personal rule by replacing the Heimwehr with his own 'brownshirts', the Front Miliz, Schuschnigg continued Dollfuss's drift towards clerical fascism by restructuring Austria as a Catholic corporate state. In this he was supported by the clergy, whose leaders had publicly and repeatedly denounced 'Jewish' Marxism, materialism, liberalism and individualism. Trade unions were suppressed, business interests given a free hand and punitive measures taken against democrats, socialists and Jews. Corporate associations were organized along professional and vocational lines. Thus Schuschnigg and the old Austrian right tried to maintain an Austria that was both fascist and independent.

But the leaders of Austrian clerical fascism were trapped by an unavoidable contradiction. In Germany, as we shall see, the Nazis were to use Germany's industrial and human resources to resolve, through conquest and exploitation, the social and economic problems of the Depression years. Tiny and bankrupt Austria had no such resources. Only a greater Germany had the power to subdue the Slavs and make Germans once again supreme in the old imperial territories. The very success of the Austrian right had destroyed the only domestic voice raised against Anschluss, that of the socialist left. More Austrians began to see Hitler as he himself had seen Schönerer thirty years before: as the potential saviour of the embattled German *Volk* community of central and eastern Europe. The Austrian government watched apprehensively as more and more Nazis emerged in the former strongholds of anti-Nazi Austrian ultra-conservatism: associations of landowners, artisans and white-collar workers, the judicial and teaching professions, and the corporate heads of communications, transport and utilities. Meanwhile, the German Embassy and Austrian businessmen provided funds for the growing demand for Anschluss.

Hitler could not move, however, until Mussolini's opposition to German expansion could be neutralized. The chance came when Allied sanctions against Mussolini for his invasion of Ethiopia, and. German-Italian cooperation in Spain, gave rise to the Rome-Berlin Axis of 1936. When Schuschnigg attempted to hold a plebiscite in 1938 to decide whether or not Austria should remain independent of Germany, Hitler had the pretext he had been waiting for – especially since the plebiscite was manipulated to aid Schuschnigg's hope for a favourable vote. Expressing his gratitude to Mussolini for raising no objections, Hitler made another major effort to realize the Austro-Pan-German ideals of his youth. Austria was invaded and occupied on 12 March 1938.

Post-war Germany provided an ideal environment for the re-volutionary conservatives of the radical right. For the first time since Bismarck took office, Germany's reactionary élites were threatened by the liberal and leftward transformation of politics and society that they had always feared. Having lost the war, the former leaders of Germany also lost the means to stave off these changes by military success, and were forced to work within the limits of parliamentary democracy. More than ever before, Germany's ultra-conservatives needed the votes of the masses to maintain the old system. This the Nazis were able to provide by mobilizing the social discontents of the lower middle classes. The trauma of the war, the economic chaos of inflation and depression, the fear of socialism and Bolshevism – all these helped persuade millions of voters and highly-placed con-servatives that the Nazis constituted the last line of defence against liberal and radical agitation, votes for social welfare, land-reform, demilitarization, proletarian gains and the permanent shift of power away from the inheritors of Bismarck's legacy. Finally, the harsh terms of the Treaty of Versailles aided the German right. It seemed the duty of patriots to support those who possessed both the will and the potential force to reverse those terms: the Nazis and the German army, which was closely allied with the radical right from 1919 onwards in spite of its apolitical posture.

As for Nazi ideology, neither clinical psychology, Teutonic philosophy nor unique German proclivities need be called upon to explain it. Hitler could draw upon ultra-conservative ideas that were decades old, ideas created by a multitude of intellectuals in other nations as well as in Germany. We have seen how the direct line of influence was Hitler's exposure to Austro-Pan-Germanism during his youth in Linz and Vienna.

The upsurge of semi-fascist activities after the 1914–18 war owed much to right-wing veterans who, retaining their uniforms and arms, fought to defend Germany's frontiers against Slavs and Bolsheviks. Often joined by bourgeois students, these para-military 'free corps' also used violence to break up the meetings of pacifists, democrats, socialists, striking workers and radical peasant groups. Hitler was one of many street-corner demagogues who, paid by the army and provided with illegal arms, mobilized public opinion by impassioned

43–44   Pro-Nazi posters for the German parliamentary elections of 1928. Left, 'Should he grow even fatter?' The German common man 'Michael' is crushed by the bloated figure of Jewish capitalism. Right, 'Against hunger and despair! Vote Hitler!', design by Mjölnir.

and skilful harangues. Their theme was monotonously similar: the Versailles Treaty was an Allied-Jewish plot to destroy Germany; the socialists and liberals of Weimar who signed and enforced the Treaty terms were criminals and traitors; the German army had not lost the war, but had been 'stabbed in the back' by home-front slackers, Bolshevik-inspired strikers and Jewish war-profiteers.

In 1923 the French invaded the Ruhr to put pressure on the German government to honour overdue reparations payments. This and the terrible inflation, attributed falsely by conservatives to the Treaty, inspired Hitler to imitate his hero, Mussolini, and organize a *Putsch* against the government of Bavaria. He was joined by no less a figure than Field-Marshal Ludendorff, the former commander of the German armies on the western front. Police bullets ended the revolt, but the sentences meted out for this act of high treason indicated only too clearly where the sympathies of the conservative establishment lay. Ludendorff got off scot-free; Hitler spent some months in a comfortable prison. The failure of the 1923 *Putsch* taught Hitler a valuable lesson. Before they could seize power, the Nazis would have to demonstrate their usefulness to the army and conservative élites by gaining sufficient votes to make it possible to reverse the liberal policies of the Weimar Republic by legal methods, and hence without risk of Allied intervention or proletarian uprisings.

After his release from prison, Hitler entered the contest for office that he had formerly despised. From 1924 to 1929, however, the Nazis were reduced to relative impotence by the end of inflation, Allied concessions on reparations, and general prosperity. Only after 1929, when the Great Depression shattered and polarized German society once again, did the Nazis gain the votes they needed.

Support for the Nazis came from a variety of sources. Self-employed small businessmen, always economically vulnerable, their markets now eroded by the Depression, moved to the radical right to express resentment at Weimar pro-unionism, which forced them to pay their employees union rates. Such men, together with their families and their employees, defined their position in society by an ethic which stressed hard work, deferred consumption and the accumulation of enough savings to give their children the education which would prevent them from sinking into the proletariat. Inflation and the Depression mocked their efforts by wiping out their savings and shops. Not surprisingly, during these years they deserted the middle-class parties to which they had previously belonged, because only Hitler seemed to possess the determination and shock troops needed to smash the trade unions and socialism, end Weimar's social welfare schemes and protect shopkeepers from (often Jewish-owned) large retail outlets.

At the same time, the Nazis needed the funds of corporate industry to finance their political campaigns. To this end, Hitler used the old (and false) distinction between parasitic 'Jewish' finance capital with its international allegiance, and the patriotic primary producers of 'Aryan' corporate industry. Unlike the radical right in other Western nations, the Nazis could divert the blame for the Depression away from the structural weaknesses of capitalism by invoking the reparations clauses of the Treaty of Versailles. To the confused, unsophisticated and desperate small proprietors and clerks of town and village, the Nazis made ultra-patriotism, anti-Semitism and forceful solutions seem the only way to restore stability in the chaos of the 1930s.

Another major source of Nazi votes were the employees of the vast and growing bureaucracies of corporations and government. They had long since formed white-collar associations which excluded Jews, whose competition they feared, and cultivated respectability and non-proletarian status. Their lives of strict obedience to superiors and petty harshness towards inferiors reinforced their identity with the titled officials of the upper hierarchies of management and administration. Firm in their belief in the superior efficiency of business and bureaucratic experts, they despised the vote-seeking demagogues of the Weimar Republic.

The smaller the town or village, the more rural the area, the larger the percentage of the Nazi vote. Correspondingly, the sturdy peasant farmer or rural craftsman was the Nazi ideal-type. Praising such men as living bastions of the old order, the Nazis promised to protect them from the inroads of modern technology and the terrible burden of indebtedness. Hundreds of thousands of mortgage foreclosures had wiped out the ancestral lands of the peasant on his family farm, making a mockery of his back-breaking toil. The Weimar Republic

45–46 The German peasant as source of life and as source of reaction. Left, *The Sower*, by the right-wing artist Oscar Martin-Amorbach (1897–   ). Right, satire from the left: *Industrial Peasants*, by Georg Scholz, oil and collage on wood, 1920.

did nothing substantial to stop this human misery, and too many Marxists shrugged it off as the inevitable result of the advance of capitalism. The Nazis offered to halt foreclosures, extend easy credit and maintain price subsidies for the small farmer. Anti-Semitism pre-dated the Nazis by decades in rural areas. The simple and strong Christian faith of the peasant contributed much to it, but so also did the peasant's perception of what he took to be the exploiting economic role of the Jew in the countryside – as cattle-dealer, money-lender and mortgage-holder.

Uneducated and unsophisticated, the rural villager did not understand that all were part of an economic system dominated by good Nordic and Aryan financial circles in Berlin, Hamburg and Munich. During the hard times of the late nineteenth century, demagogues much like Hitler had often stimulated anti-Semitic riots in rural Germany. Among those who tended most strongly to vote for the Nazis were peasants forced by hard times to leave their lands and villages and seek work in the big cities. In symbol, ritual and speeches, Hitler and the Nazis mobilized accumulated frustrations by evoking nostalgic and noble images of rural life and castigating the moral permissiveness and alienation of urban society.

Unlike the radical right elsewhere, the Nazis found it relatively easy to gain support from the traditional German conservative élites. Naturally enough, these élites preferred their own party (DNVP), which was also ultra-conservative, ultra-nationalist and élitist, to the un-cultured lower-class followers of a disreputable rabble-rouser like Hitler. But by 1932 traditionalists had little choice, for the votes of the combined non-Nazi right had dropped from 28 per cent to less than 10 per cent of the national total, while the Nazi vote had soared to 35 per cent.

Conservatives were all the more fearful because the combined votes of the Marxist Social Democrats and Communists hovered around 34 per cent. Sharing, if in more moderate form, Hitler's basic ideas, but too 'respectable' and élitist to outbid him in the streets, leaders of traditional conservative groups hoped to use Nazi votes and violence to overturn Weimar for their own ends. The threats conservatives faced were immense. If Weimar democracy survived the Depression, the power of Bismarck's heirs would shift permanently to the voting masses. Given the electoral power, during stable years, of the democratic and reforming parties of the middle and left, this would mean attacks on the fiscal privileges of wealthy autocratic families through tax and land reforms. As for the army, even if it were freed from the restrictions of the Treaty of Versailles, it would lose its powerful voice in domestic and foreign policy and become, at long last, the instrument of civilians. Industrialists would have to learn to live with collective bargaining, strikes and perhaps even some forms of the nationalization of the means of production. Finally, the ultimate conservative goal so often stated in the party manifestos of the DNVP – a foreign policy that would provide *Lebensraum* at the expense of Slavs and Bolsheviks – would be permanently denied. Liberal and left-wing politicians did want to revise the Versailles Treaty in Germany's favour, but they were not interested in renewing the *Drang nach Osten*. For all these reasons, as Germany's leading political general, Kurt von Schleicher, once said: 'If the Nazis did not exist, it would have been necessary to invent them.'

From the start of his campaign for votes, Hitler had been able to attract contributions from small businessmen. Once convinced of the Nazi power to attract votes, important industrialists made substantial contributions to Hitler. Funds were channelled through Hjalmar Schacht and Alfred Hugenberg. Head of the DNVP, Hugenberg was also a co-director of Krupp, and owner of a vast press and film network. In return for the support of these gentlemen of means, Hitler toured the Rhineland and indicated that he would destroy the left, restrict trade-union arrogance and rearm Germany – in spite of the Versailles Treaty and the 'traitors and Jews' who ran the Weimar Republic. Hitler also reminded the chiefs of heavy industry of the vast wealth ready to be exploited in the east and in the Soviet Union.

In nations where liberalism has had significant influence, racism tends to decrease as one ascends the social and educational ladder. But in Germany the upper classes had held Jews in contempt with age-old historical consistency, and kept them out of the conservative preserves of the army, the bureaucracy and some of the white-collar professions. It has often been suggested that many German Jews felt assimilated, but assimilation is a fact, not a feeling. As we have seen, Jews were highly over-represented throughout central and eastern Europe in those professions and political groups most feared by traditional conservatives, and the call for discriminatory and punitive measures against the Jews was nothing new. Of course, it was a rare non-Nazi who wanted to murder the Jews, but the overwhelming majority of German conservatives supported some substantial denial of civil rights and had done so long before the rise of the Nazis.

In short, the traditional conservatives who aided Hitler rarely desired to follow him to the most brutal extremes. But they failed to see that Nazi brutality derived from the iron logic of their own willingness to see the tides of social change reversed by force. Rather than take responsibility for their own share of Germany's ills and attempt to resolve these ills through social reform, German conservatives preferred to put all the blame on the enemies denounced by Hitler: the Allies, the international Jewish and communist conspirators, and the domestic partisans of liberal democracy and socialism. These, the right believed, were the people responsible for Germany's economic collapse, for the class hatreds which divided the *Volk* community, for the imposition of an alien form of government designed to encourage weakness and for the consequent second-rate status of Germany in world affairs.

Thus, the Nazis succeeded in Germany because their rhetoric, programme and votes made them the champions of the reactionary, aristocratic, military and industrial establishment, and the last, desperate hope of the ultra-patriotic, economically frustrated and embittered lower middle classes.

President Hindenburg appointed Hitler chancellor in January 1933. He did so somewhat reluctantly, but on the advice of important business, political and military leaders. All were aware that, barring an inconceivable accommodation with the left, they could find no parliamentary majority without the Nazis. As storm troopers rioted outside the Reichstag, Hitler demanded full emergency powers. All but the Marxist parties voted as he demanded. Now only the army could stop him. But the military were content with Nazi rule providing only that Hitler's brownshirts (SA) were not allowed to replace the regular army as SA leaders hoped. Hitler gave them the guarantee they sought. In June 1934 Himmler's SS executed some 1,000 SA leaders. Thus when Hindenburg died in August, the army gratefully allowed Hitler to combine the offices of chancellor and president, and swore an unprecedented oath of personal allegiance to the Führer. Whatever hope non-Nazi conservatives might have had of manipulating Hitler was gone. The support of the army and his personal popularity made him invulnerable.

The dynamic totalitarianism and sweeping imperialism character-istic of Nazi rule were not arbitrary policies; they were the result of the contradictions inherent in the rule of the radical right over a country which was otherwise the most advanced in Europe. In more backward nations, such as Spain or Portugal, the interests of traditional élites could be defended by authoritarian despots with simple, if brutal, police repression. But in Germany Hitler was faced both with a vast, self-conscious and well-organized proletariat whose repression required totalitarian techniques, and with millions of middle-class citizens with high expectations and aspirations. Hitler was well aware that repression was no permanent solution. If the Depression continued in Germany, the Nazis themselves might be toppled from power. Yet Hitler could not, of course, desert his followers and work for a Nazi 'New Deal'. Moreover, if he followed the bourgeois policies of governments like those of Great Britain and France, his New Order would merely result in further economic and political stagnation. The leaders of Japan shared with the Nazis the cult of the warrior and, as racists, had nothing but scorn for the liberal notion of the right of weak nations to self-determination. By the same creed, the Nazi leadership saw in conquest the means to bring the wealth of empire to bear and end for good the economic miseries of the *Herrenvolk* at the expense of the lesser breeds of Europe and Russia.

To accomplish their policies, the Nazis needed to destroy the left and strengthen the militaristic, authoritarian and ultra-conservative elements of German society. In 1933 all political parties were accordingly disbanded, and those on the left had their assets seized and their leaders jailed. By 1935 Nazi Party members held half of all bureaucratic posts. To the annoyance of many Nazi 'old-fighters', however, this was in part because of the mass conversion of titled and middle-class Germans already in possession of such posts. No great transformation was necessary. Once the minority of democrats, socialists and Jews had been purged, the vast majority of the remaining public officials had no serious objections to either the destruction of the Weimar Republic or the attitudes of their new leaders. Indeed, senior civil servants were pleased when the Nazis gave them more authority over their inferiors, and otherwise encouraged the bureaucratic penchant for a *Beamtenstaat*, or government of experts unrestricted by liberal politicians or electorates. Lesser civil servants were kept under close government surveillance so as to ensure loyalty. As for the 'old-fighters' who were given public office, especially in the conquered territories, they were unbelievably inefficient and corrupt.

The German army was handsomely rewarded for its support and its important role in Nazi policies. From 1933 to 1938 its share of ever larger national budgets rose from 23 per cent to 74 per cent. Conscription returned in 1935, but until the massive influx of recruits after Stalingrad, the aristocracy maintained its near monopoly of the higher ranks of the officer corps. There were many senior officers who feared Hitler's grandiose plans for conquest, but the bulk of the military leadership willingly looked forward to the status and rewards they would enjoy in the battle against the inferior peoples and Bolsheviks of the east. Army units, not just the dreaded SS, willingly carried out the massive destruction of whole villages and their non-combatant populations in Poland and Russia. Hitler was well aware, however, that the army was the one institution which could resist his will. Accordingly, he replaced many top officers with his sycophants, established SS divisions directly responsible to the Party through Himmler and encouraged the promotion of young pro-Nazi officers. Indeed, after the war Hitler intended to nazify the army completely; there were to be no competitors for power in the Third Reich.

Contrary to the impression given by those who view the Nazis as an organization of lower-class rabble, the sons of aristocratic and upper middle-class families were highly over-represented in the SS leadership, as well as in the notorious murder squads, the Einsatzgruppen. Led by Hermann Göring, Nazi leaders aped the life style of the assorted princes, counts and barons who were their preferred companions. In the schools for training the future élite, Baldur von Schirach had carefully selected Aryans (appropriately called Junkers) trained in Nazi ideology, aristocratic deportment and the martial arts. Amidst the trappings of medieval décor in remote castles, Nazi youths were taught to suppress any remnants of Christian or liberal values they might possess in order to be fit to rule the eastern peoples with utter ruthlessness. These future leaders of Europe's New Order were recruited from the 'reliable classes'. Overwhelmingly, they tended to be sons of aristocrats, military officers, civil servants and white-collar workers. But Hitler did not intend to allow the old aristocracy to have any independent power in the Third Reich; they would either become one with the Party leadership or be replaced after the war. Nor would there be any monarchist revival; Hitler and Goebbels intended to murder any princely families who survived the war.

The German judiciary had always been anti-Weimar and proud of its Prussian values. Swiftly converted to Nazi uses, the bench more or less willingly served leaders whose attitudes were only an extreme extension of their own ultra-conservatism. Consequently, by the onset of the war, the powers of the Nazi public prosecutor were such that, where political or racial 'undesirables' were concerned, judges were simply told what sentences to hand down and were required to admit as evidence the results of Gestapo torture. In Nazi training camps, lawyers were taught the nineteenth-century conservative view of crime: that habitual crime was genetically determined and bore no relationship to unfavourable social circumstances. Punishment and eugenic policies, not reform and rehabilitation, were to be the norm. During the Third Reich, habitual offenders were likely to end up in death-camps. The Nazis also carried nineteenth-century prudery to brutal extremes. Homosexuals, held to be literally degenerate, were savagely persecuted. For 'race defilers', usually Jews or Slavs who were alleged to have had sexual relationships with Aryans, the penalty was death.

The Nazi belief in the superiority of rural life and the importance of the small farmer, artisan and shopkeeper had led some Party leaders to hope for extensive legislation to aid such groups. However, a serious reversal of the trend towards large units and complex technologies would not only have harmed important Nazi supporters, but would also have hindered economic recovery and left the needs of the powerful military machine unmet. Where the influence of the wealthy and economic efficiency were not primary considerations, the Nazis did help the small proprietors in the towns and countryside whose support had been so vital in the early days of the movement. Small businessmen were often favoured when government contracts were issued. Guilds were given more control over their members, masters' examinations were again required for craftsmen who hoped to open their own shops, and non-licensed working artisans were punished.

But economic rationalization was not halted. Only those artisans and small shops survived which were isolated and rural, or which met the needs of larger firms by sub-contracting. Party ideologists like Gottfried Feder, who had hoped to halt the spread of corporate industrialism, were removed from policy-making positions and given the task of presiding over a revived medieval guild pageantry intended to confer pride and status on the artisans. But the Nazis did extend easier credit terms to small businessmen, and by legislation they effectively slowed down the previously rapid growth of large chain- and department stores. The brutal 'aryanization' of Jewish property enabled many a small businessman and Party member to turn a quick profit.

Much was done by the Nazis to help the small peasant proprietor so idealized in ultra-conservative doctrine. Many family farms were designated as *Erbhöfe*. These could not be mortgaged or sold and had to be passed on intact to the eldest son, who would also inherit the title of 'noble of race and soil'. Small farmers often had their markets and prices protected, and easy credit terms were arranged to help avoid the terrors of mass bankruptcy which at that time was the fate of millions of small farmers in Western nations. Apart from the favoured *Erbhöfe*, however, thousands of small farms did go under in Germany and peasant indebtedness increased. Large landowners, often titled, fared better. They dominated the Reich Farmers' Association which exercised a powerful influence over the extensive agrarian controls introduced by the Nazis, and their superior productivity made them vital to a régime which aimed at self-sufficiency in foodstuffs. Some Nazi ideologists had hoped to prevent the spread of industrial urbanization by damming the flow of displaced farmers to town and factory, or at least by locating plants in rural settings. But, as in all other respects, the true Nazi social revolution had to await foreign conquests. Millions of Nordic peasants would then be resettled in the rich agrarian territories of the east, there to supervise the labour of Slavs in lands whose principal cities were to be razed to the ground.

Much as they may have wished to do so, the Nazis could not afford to return to the pre-industrial principles they espoused or maintain the 'little man' at the cost of productivity and economic growth. Except for a few rare individuals who resisted the Nazis or failed to cooperate with rearmament plans, the income of those who already owned the most capital or property increased. Net corporate profits went up fourfold between 1933 and 1938; the incomes of business managers rose by some 45 per cent; and shareholders enjoyed increasing profits. As in Vichy France and Fascist Italy, the rhetoric of the corporate state disguised the fact that basic economic decisions were made by big business leaders and sympathetic Party officials. Workers were not consulted. Hitler did have some difficulties with Schacht and the steel magnates of the Ruhr, who had assumed that Hitler's arms build-up was intended merely to stimulate the economy. By 1937 they wanted to re-tool for the production of consumer goods for export. Hitler replaced Schacht, remarking that the financial wizard was not a real Nazi, and the economy was put under more direct Party control. In a meeting that same year, Hitler informed his military and diplomatic chiefs that German arms were intended for conquest in the east, not merely as a pump-priming device. From 1936 to 1939 German industry expanded at a historically unprecedented rate, although the mobilization of the economy for total war was not to come until Hitler's *Blitzkrieg* tactics failed at Stalingrad. Once war broke out, German industrialists were eager to seize the assets of foreign firms and employ slave labour. However, there is much to indicate that, had Hitler won the war, the basic economic institutions would have been brought under full Nazi control. Increasingly, Party leaders directed production. The organization intended for the future was symbolized by the Hermann Göring Works, a vast international combine with branches in the conquered territories.

Why did German workers cooperate with a régime which had destroyed their unions and political representatives? Partly, of course, because Hitler's control of army and police, and his willingness to use any means necessary to control social discontent, made effective resistance impossible. It is crucial to note, however, that Hitler was the only Western leader to end unemployment. Six million Germans were unemployed in 1930; in 1938 there was a labour shortage. This was accomplished in a variety of ways. The Nazis stimulated the economy by credits to heavy industry and by guaranteeing Wehrmacht arms purchases. Previously unemployed workers and new entrants into the labour market were sent to compulsory labour camps. There they were paid subsistence wages to clear lands, build roads and service projects which increased Germany's war potential but did not compete with the private sector. With the abolition of trade unions, wage rates could be kept substantially below pre-Depression levels and, to the further delight of employers, piece-rates and longer hours could be introduced in the name of maximum production for the might of the Fatherland.

The highly skilled and privileged blue-collar workers of the steel and construction industries fared well under the Nazis, but workers of lesser skills took wage cuts. In order to prevent the independent mobilization of worker discontent, a vast Labour Front was organized under Robert Ley. Its function was to prevent workers from forming separate unions which would respond to their specific demands. Even the Nazi state needed more than sheer force where tens of millions were involved. Thus workers were organized along para-military lines and bombarded with the slogans of *Volk* rhetoric: the glory of the Fatherland, the nobility of toil, the need for class unity, and the comradeship of managerial 'Führers' with worker-soldiers in the 'battle of labour' to free Germany from foreign oppression. As Ley once indicated to an employers' association, one could demand anything from a worker who thought of himself as a fellow comrade-in-arms. Naturally, workers had no way of knowing that corporate profits and managerial incomes were soaring. Nevertheless, Hitler feared worker discontent, and here too he found in conquest the appropriate policy. In the Thousand Year Reich, skilled and highly paid Nordic workers would supervise the slave labour of eastern Europe's *Untermenschen*. Thus German arms would guarantee that the German proletariat would remain for ever invulnerable to left-wing ideologies.

Conforming to traditional conservative doctrine, the Nazis hoped to be able to confine women to home, family, pregnancy and those few tasks, such as nursing, which suited the supposedly unique feminine qualities of maternal tenderness and concern for the family. The liberated female of the Weimar Republic was an abomination to conservatives; to grant votes to women, as was done in 1920, was regarded as sheer desecration of the home by conservatives and Nazis alike. But the needs of war brought an increasingly larger percentage of women into the work force. Once again, the appropriate changes could come only with the end of the war. Then women would be restored to their proper functions. Meanwhile, the best the Nazis could do was to keep women out of politics, the civil service and higher education, and channel them into the less skilled and less lucrative tasks of farm and factory. Women were not given equal pay for equal work, and men were the first to be promoted.

The Nazi Woman's Association promoted the official image of womanhood: the Nordic ideal of shy but sensual modesty, spartan

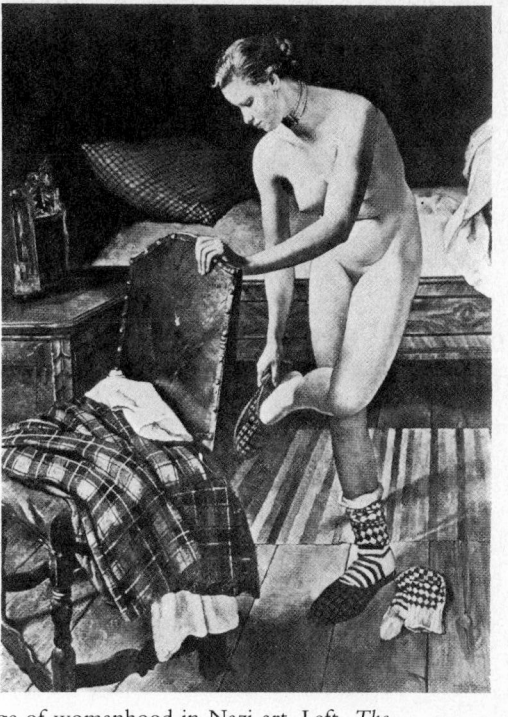

47–48   The cult of virility and the image of womanhood in Nazi art. Left, *The Discus Thrower*, by Lothar Bechstein (1884–1936). Right, *Peasant Venus*, by Sepp Hilz, 1938.

tastes, peasant styles and physical fitness. The leaders of the official Motherhood Cult castigated abortion as sabotage and rewarded fertility with medals and cash. As for women's rights, Hitler himself is said to have insisted that in the Third Reich every woman would be guaranteed a husband. Through his *Lebensborn* programme, Heinrich Himmler encouraged carefully selected 'Nordic' women to have intercourse with SS men, and comfortable homes were established for such unwed mothers. Recent evidence suggests that Himmler may have had thousands of foreign children of the right skull measurements kidnapped to add to Germany's breeding-stock. Some of the Nazi leaders were quite prepared to make personal sacrifices. They suggested that all Party members might be required to take two or three wives. All these measures were designed to ensure the genetic quality of the future racial community of the Reich. In this and in many other aspects of Nazi ideology and practice, the influence of conservative interpretations of social Darwinism is striking.

Although there were some noble exceptions and even martyrs, the hierarchies of the Catholic and Lutheran clergy in Germany adapted themselves to Nazi rule without serious trouble. Church leaders in central Europe had long held ultra-conservative views, and many a pulpit had resounded with denunciations of the secular liberalism of the West, 'Jewish' materialism and the Bolshevik antichrist. Catholic leaders welcomed Hitler's support of Franco and his invasion of Russia. Some bishops did protest against Hitler's euthanasia programme, the murder of innocent hostages and the extermination of former Jews who had converted to Catholicism.

In spite of its general passivity, the Nazis saw Christianity as a potential rival for German loyalties. Hitler banned Christian youth groups and curbed the educational influence of the Church. With the advent of war, Hitler no longer muted the voices of those Nazis who had hoped all along to rid Germany of 'Jew-corrupted' Christianity and to replace it with the neo-pagan sun, nature and Wotan cults of which the ultra-right, including Himmler himself, had long been devotees. To this end Nazi sacraments were invented and the swastika replaced the cross as the symbol of transcendental religion. The counsel of meekness and humility preached by Jesus, a 'Jewish coward', was to give way to the ideal of the sacredness of death in battle for the racial community. Appropriate ceremonials and eternal memorials to German battle dead were created.

During the Third Reich, cultural activities served to reinforce conservative attitudes, communicate Nazi ideology and detach people from their potentially dangerous individual or class perspectives. Hitler's speeches and the numerous Nazi holidays and ceremonies were ritualistic, massive and theatrical set-pieces, designed to overwhelm that which is merely human and to subvert the ever-fragile link between reason and evidence. The impact of Nazi pageantry can best be experienced in Leni Riefenstahl's documentary film of the Nuremberg Party rally of 1934, *Triumph of the Will*. To a majestic Wagnerian rendering of the Nazi Party song, Hitler's plane soars over the medieval rooftops of the city – a symbol of the determination of the revolutionary ultra-right to defend the values of pre-industrial Germany with the latest in modern technology. Throughout the film, the spectator is overwhelmed by seemingly endless massed columns of marching warriors, accompanied by streams of flags, torches and Nazi regalia. Uniforms, on

49 The impact of Nazi ceremonial: Storm Troopers' Day at the Great Nazi Congress, Nuremberg, 13 September 1936. View showing one of the immense papier-mâché German eagles erected in the Luitpoldarena.

civilians and non-civilians alike, serve to merge the identity of the individual with the unity of the *Volk* militant. Carefully selected crowds chant to the slogans of impassioned orators, finally to fall under the hypnotic sway of Hitler himself.

Traditional tyrants are content with silence; totalitarian rulers must manufacture approval for their dynamic policies. To this end the Nazis made active use of school, press and radio. Elementary schoolteachers in Germany had traditionally been fervent supporters of the ultra-nationalist right. After appropriate purges, they willingly presented Nazi dogma by the preferred teaching methods of autocracy. Lectures, passive notetaking and memorization replaced the permissive educational experimentation encouraged by the Weimar Republic. The Nazi Party paper, the *Völkische Beobachter*, became the first national newspaper in German history, its circulation swollen by the subscriptions of those who wished to curry favour with the regime. Modelled on Hitler's harangues, its editorials avoided any attempt to persuade through rational argument. This would have meant stating alternative views and leaving room for doubt and the free play of intellect. Above all, the Nazis exploited the power of the radio. Government subsidies financed a vast increase in radio sets. Public loudspeakers, often located in places of work, led to communal listening-breaks designed to ensure that the slogans of the right would become a part of the collective daily experience in ways that private reading could not accomplish.

The Nazis detested and purged *avant-garde* culture and its practitioners. Nineteenth-century art forms and ultra-conservative content were dominant during the Third Reich. Medieval Germany was idealized and her ancient racial struggles filled stage and screen. Countless epics of 'blood and soil' glorified peasant life, rustic values and the ordinary German – honest, industrious and traditionally duped by wily and ruthless aliens of doubtful genes. The soldier, the pilot and the athlete were repeatedly portrayed, for they symbolized the virile conquest of mere physical limitations by energy, will and spirit. Leni Riefenstahl's film of the 1936 Olympics, *Olympiad*, projects this Nazi ideal with compelling subtlety. In music, Hitler's favourite Wagnerian strains were used for filmed and staged evocations of the German past and the German character. Jazz and the saxophone were denounced as decadent and 'negroid'. The hearty rhythms of the communal village *Volk* dance were encouraged in place of the overt sensuality and individualistic exhibitionism of ballroom dancing.

Not surprisingly, upper-class conservatives and the lower middle-class masses tended to prefer older and more familiar varieties of realism in art. Like the Kaiser before him, Hitler personally detested Post-Impressionism; he denounced it as the degenerate creation of a Jewish and Marxist Paris. The Nazis enforced conservative tastes in art as a means of reinforcing their social controls. Expressionism displayed the private feelings and perceptions of the individual;

Cubism stressed the relativity of perception to the varying perspectives of time, space and subject. Taken together, both movements threatened the vulgar realism of the masses, encouraged what the Nazis could only perceive as anarchic individualism and denied the Nazi claim to simple and unvarying truth. The Nazis burned not only books, but also some 4,000 canvases representing nearly all the great names of modern art. As Hitler himself pronounced, nature's colours and forms were to be copied without distortion; art was to follow ideology. The favourite subjects of Nazi painting and sculpture were steely-eyed soldiers, thick-bodied peasants and awesomely-proportioned women – all advancing into a heroic future with grim determination, tensed muscles and lofted torch, banner, hammer or weapon. Human dimensions were overawed by Nazi architecture which was dominated by monumental tomb-like structures with facades and porticos supported by vast columns marching in military rhythms. The future palaces of the SS governors of the east were to be stark and gloomy fortresses modelled on imaginary medieval forms. As befitted Nazi dreams of a rural society, there would be no great cities in the east; the few administrative centres necessary for government were to be designed without a trace of individuality or spontaneity.

In moral behaviour, philosophy and even science, the Nazis insisted that truth must be consistent, final and absolute, as in the days before pragmatism and relativism. With some inconsistency, Nazi ideologists held that truth must be German as well. Germans must behave at all times according to a fixed code of ethics and right conduct, and ignore any considerations of the varieties of individual experience, personality or situation. The liberal nations of the West might surrender to the various 'Einsteins' with their 'Jewish' attack on absolute truth and common sense, but not the German people. For the Nazis, pragmatism and relativism weakened determination and purpose, which were strong only if based on the certainties of absolute knowledge. Liberal pragmatists were unable to act decisively, for they were constantly held back by their view that truth was relative to transient conditions or situations, and subject to the impact of new evidence and fresh experience. The cultural and philosophical attitudes denounced by the Nazis were repudiated because they threatened the certainties and dogmas of a monolithic, totalitarian ideology.

The Nazi murder of nearly 6 million Jews is a horror unmatched in modern history. To this one must add something like another 4 million murdered non-combatants, including political and racial 'undesirables', civilian hostages, prisoners of war and the inhabitants of thousands of eastern villages which stood in the path of the German juggernaut. As we have seen, there were very few non-Nazi conservatives who wanted the Jews exterminated. But there was a conservative consensus to deny Jews civil rights, bar them from important positions in society, or drive them out of Germany altogether. To support the Nazis, however, was to surrender responsibility for setting any limits to barbarism. Moreover, it is impossible to believe that the systematic slaughter of so many millions in less than three years was simply the act of a few thousand Nazi fanatics. It involved the knowledge and the active participation of a vast number of bureaucrats, judges, lawyers, diplomats and soldiers. For the truly sincere Nazi, guilt feelings could be more easily muted. Ideology and his superiors had taught him that the slaughter was a moral deed which would cleanse and purify Europe of the degenerate enemies of humanity. Death, like imperialism, was a major social policy of the Third Reich. At first Jews were banned from the professions, then their property was seized, and finally, in June 1942, mass gassing began at Buchenwald. By the end of the war a people and its culture had disappeared from Europe.

50   Atrocities committed during the Second World War in Yugoslavia by Nazis and the fascist Ustaše.

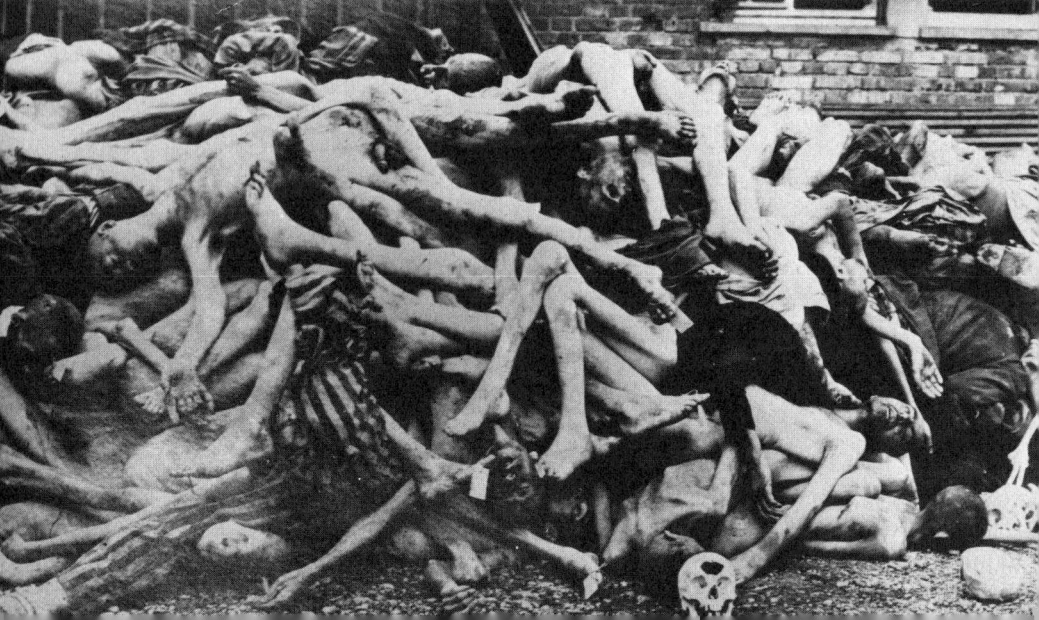

By 1937 rearmament, the forced austerity of the workers and credit manipulation could do no more to maintain full employment or adequate living standards in Germany. If the economy were not to stagnate, it would be necessary to generate more purchasing power and compete through exports in world markets. But Hitler could see no reason to follow liberal policies of peaceful competition for world markets. Germany would again face the possibility of depression and unemployment, and the dynamic New Order of the Nazis would have proved as stagnant as Weimar and Western liberalism. Hitler preferred to conquer raw materials, productive capacity and human resources. As we have already noted, in 1937 Hitler informed his generals and diplomats that they must prepare themselves for the final race-struggle for *Lebensraum* in the east and Russia. He emphasized that no mercy was to be shown. The ruling élites of the east would be exterminated, and the indigenous population reduced by tens of millions. Only those who could be of some use to the Germans would be permitted to live. German dominance and security, as well as the future of Nordic mankind, would be assured. There is no doubt that Hitler intended to carry out this brutal vision; indeed he had already begun to do so before the end of the war.

Nevertheless, hindsight should not lead us to take the path of easy moralizing and to condemn the policy of appeasement followed by Great Britain and France. There was no precedent for Nazi brutality and totalitarian imperialism. Like their electorates, the leaders of Great Britain and France were trapped by their own past experience in ways that made appeasement seem a reasonable policy. We now know that once Hitler had rearmed Germany, only military action could have stopped him. But until Hitler dismembered Czechoslovakia in March 1939, it was tempting for Western leaders to hope that, at the worst, Hitler intended only to tear up the Versailles Treaty and gather all ethnic Germans into the Reich. Western opinion had long condemned the Versailles Treaty as unfair and unenforceable; moreover, it was and is a liberal dogma that ethnic groups have a right to self-determination. Finally, Hitler counted on a swift decision through *Blitzkrieg* tactics. The politicians and the public in Great Britain and France feared a repetition of the horrors of 1914–18, compounded by the gassing and bombing of civilians on a grand scale. Western leaders needed a negotiated settlement; Hitler needed war.

Thus Hitler manipulated events within the limits of the assumptions of traditional diplomacy, assumptions which neutralized an armed Western response until the invasion of Poland. When Hitler rearmed Germany, he was merely exercising what was almost unanimously agreed to be the right of a sovereign state. When he sent German troops to remilitarize the Rhineland in 1936, he was following the normal policy of exercising military control over national territories. Great Britain and France could hardly have been expected to challenge this action by armed force, especially in view of public apathy. As for Anschluss in 1938, most Austrians welcomed it. Austria was already under fascist rule, though of a different variety, Mussolini was neutral and Western electorates showed little evidence of willingness to support another world war to prevent Germans from annexing Germans. When Hitler demanded that the Czechs turn over the Sudeten Germans to the Reich, the same principle held back a West conscious of its own military weakness and aware that the Sudeten Germans were overwhelmingly pro-Nazi. Excluding the left, the Munich agreement found Europeans vastly relieved; President Roosevelt expressed his pleasure in a note to the Canadian Prime Minister, Mackenzie King. But when Hitler took his revenge on the hated Bohemians of his youth and dismembered Czechoslovakia in March 1939, his real intentions became clear. Western leaders and their electorates performed a dramatic about-face. At the end of the month, Chamberlain issued his famous guarantee: Great Britain would come to the aid of Poland should the Polish government decide that its independence was threatened by the acts of any foreign power. The United States offered no support.

Thus Poland was offered a blank cheque, though as far as immediate or direct military action in eastern Europe was concerned, Great Britain and France were incapable of action and knew it. The Soviet Union had access to Poland, and in accord with its anti-fascist policies had previously expressed some willingness to cooperate with the Western powers in aid of Czechoslovakia. But British and French leaders were not enthusiastic about having Bolsheviks as allies. Indeed, there were some who hoped that Stalin and Hitler might dispose of each other while the West remained uninvolved. Western military experts were nearly unanimous in their opinion that Stalin's purges had made the Red Army incapable of resisting the Germans for more than a few months. In any event, the head of the authoritarian and right-wing régime in Poland, Colonel Beck, would never allow the Russian army to enter Poland even to help against the Germans. Finally, Stalin himself could see little reason to shed Russian blood merely to help Western capitalists uphold the independence of an extremely anti-Bolshevik neighbour. Stalin was willing to consider an alliance with the Western powers, but only for a price. He expected military control of the Baltic states and territorial and political concessions in other areas of eastern Europe. Even if British and French leaders had approved, they could hardly have persuaded their electorates to engage in a moral crusade to prevent one dictator from seizing what they were prepared to grant to another.

Hitler alone knew exactly what he was doing. Thus he could easily neutralize any potential grand alliance by seeming to pay Stalin's price. On 23 August 1939 leaders of the totalitarian right and left met to sign the Nazi-Soviet Non-Aggression Pact. Secret clauses promised the return to Russia of territories lost to Poland and Romania in 1919 and 1920, as well as control of the Baltic states and other concessions. Hitler then proceeded to put pressure on Beck to make revisions in the Versailles Treaty favourable to the Germans. He assumed that the British would now see that the situation was hopeless and urge Beck to yield as they had done in the case of the Czechs. How could Poland hope to remain obdurate when confronted with a united Germany and Russia, and under pressure from its own allies? But the old combination no longer worked. Great Britain and France stood by their guarantee. As military men often do, Beck overestimated his capacity to hold off the Germans; but few non-German military leaders had any notion of the power of *Blitzkrieg*. Even so, Beck's allies had raised false hopes. In spite of their high-minded guarantees, neither Great Britain nor France had plans for an offensive in the west to relieve pressure on Poland. On 1 September 1939 Hitler invaded Poland; two days later Great Britain and France declared war. Hitler was surprised but not upset; sooner or later he would have had to neutralize the Western powers so as to have a free hand in Russia. Their action could only slow him down.

The tactics of *Blitzkrieg* suited both the German need to avoid a long or total war, and a social movement which stressed heroic vitality and daring. The invention of the tank had robbed the defensive of the superiority it had enjoyed during the First World

War. Now artillery, air strikes and shock troops could storm enemy weak points, followed closely by swift armoured columns of tanks and motorized infantry. Fanning out over the enemy countryside without stopping to build fixed defensive positions, such columns could break the communications and supply lines of the enemy, and the morale of his confused troops. The subjugation of Poland took less than a month, Russia seizing her share. In the spring of 1940 Norway, Denmark and Holland surrendered in a matter of days. On 15 May 1940 German tanks broke through in southern Belgium above the Maginot Line, and headed for the Channel coast behind the rear of the main French and British armies. The Allies could not counter this blow effectively because their armour, supply, communications and thinking were still tied to the static positional warfare of 1914–18. By 28 May the British were preparing to flee the Continent; the French surrendered on 16 June. When Göring could not guarantee air superiority against the RAF, Hitler decided against invading Great Britain. Great Britain was, in any case, reduced to inefficient bombing raids and the hope that a truly great power might come to her aid. Hitler turned to his ultimate goal, the conquest of Russia.

Had Russia fallen, Great Britain would have been helpless and the United States, in all probability, would not have been willing to make the immense sacrifices necessary to conquer a Europe dominated by Germany from the Atlantic Ocean to central Asia. On 22 June 1941 the Germans stormed into Russia with 4 million men, 3,000 tanks and 5,000 aircraft. But, like the lightning strokes of Japan in south-east Asia, Hitler's swift advances into Russia served only to disguise the vital imbalance of forces which *Blitzkrieg* tactics could not counter in the long run. After the Japanese attack at Pearl Harbor and the successful Russian defence a thousand miles within her own borders, the outcome was inevitable. The combined human and material resources of the Soviet Union and the United States far outweighed the resources of Germany, Italy and Japan. The tide began to turn at Midway in June 1942, at El Alamein in October and, most decisively of all, at Stalingrad in the winter of 1942–43. The invasion of Normandy in the summer of 1944 enabled the United States to bring its vast productive potential to bear; by late summer Soviet troops were in eastern Europe. By 9 May 1945 the war in Europe was over.

The price for defeating the legions of the radical right was immense, and the bulk of it was paid by Russia. Of over 30 million Europeans who died in the Second World War, at least 17 million were Russian. Some 6 million Poles died, most of them Jewish; 3 million non-Polish eastern Europeans perished. Four and a half million Germans, 600,000 Frenchmen, 400,000 citizens of the United Kingdom, 400,000 Italians, 300,000 Americans and 200,000 Dutchmen all paid the final price.

Pan-Germanism and its Nazi variation were utterly destroyed by the war. Eleven million Germans fled or were driven out of eastern Europe when faced with the prospect of falling into the hands of the Red Army and local resistance groups. Eastern Germany, including the ancient bastion of ultra-conservatism, East Prussia, was taken from Germany and handed over to Communist rule. The power of the Soviet Union, especially after it acquired nuclear weapons, meant that German conservatives and right-wing radicals, even if they came to power, could never again hope to renew their vision of a Teutonic east. The chances of a right-wing revival were small. The autocratic élites who had dominated Germany before Weimar, and had subsequently helped Hitler to power, were crushed and scattered. Hitler's lower middle-class supporters had gained nothing but misery from the war years. Vichy also had fallen with the Nazis, as had Austrian fascism.

After 1945 there would still be many who felt nostalgia for the traditional values of a now dead social order. There would even be those who longed once again to hear the iron tread of the radical right. But with very few exceptions, in western Europe as well as in the United States and Great Britain, all significant political decision-making was now in the hands of liberals of the right, centre or left. What we call conservatism in Europe would increasingly become, as in the United States, ossified nineteenth-century classical liberalism with some remnants of an older cultural tradition. The unintended consequences of the conservatives' last stand against social moderni-zation, liberal democracy and some measure of social reform were the disasters of war. The history of European conservatism had ended.

SELECT BIBLIOGRAPHY

*Asterisks have been used to indicate works of special significance

GENERAL

Cobban, Alfred, *Edmund Burke and the Revolt against the Eighteenth Century*, London, 1929

Dimier, L., *Les Maîtres de la contre-révolution au dix-neuvième siècle*, Paris, 1907

Droz, Jacques, *Restaurations et révolutions, 1815–1871*, Paris, 1953

Hales, E.E.Y., *The Catholic Church in the Modern World*, London, 1958

— *Pio Nono*, London and New York, 1954

Horowitz, I.L., *Radicalism and the Revolt against Reason*, London, 1961

Huntington, Samuel P., 'Conservatism as an Ideology', *American Political Science Review* LI, No 2, June 1957, pp. 454–73

Kann, Robert A., *The Problem of Restoration*, Berkeley, 1968

Kirk, Russel, *The Conservative Mind*, Chicago, 1960

Kolnai, Aurel, 'Gegenrevolution', *Kölner Vierteljahrshefte für Soziologie* X, Nos 1, 2, 1931–32, pp. 171–99, 295–319

*Lafore, Laurence, *The Long Fuse: An Interpretation of the Origins of World War I*, Philadelphia, 1965

Lipset, Seymour Martin, *Political Man*, New York, 1960

*Mannheim, Karl, *Essays on Sociology and Social Psychology*, London and New York, 1953

— *Essays on the Sociology of Knowledge*, London and New York, 1952

May, Arthur J., *The Age of Metternich, 1815–1848*, New York, 1963

*Mayer, Arno, *Dynamics of Counterrevolution in Europe*, New York, 1971

— *Politics and the Diplomacy of Peacemaking: Containment and Counterrevolution at Versailles*, New York, 1967

McClosky, Herbert, 'Conservatism and Personality', *American Political Science Review* LII, No 1, 1958, pp. 27–45

Meisel, James, *Counterrevolution: How Revolutions Die*, New York, 1966

Muhlenfeld, Hans, *Politik ohne Wunschbilder: Die Konservative Aufgabe unserer Zeit*, Munich, 1927

Naef, Werner, *Zur Geschichte der Heiligen Allianz*, Bern, 1928

Nolte, Ernst, *Three Faces of Fascism*, London, 1965

Pirenne, J.H., *La Sainte-Alliance*, 2 vols, Neuchâtel, 1946–49

Robertson, Priscilla, *Revolutions of 1848: A Social History*, Princeton, 1952

*Rogger, Hans, and E. Weber (eds), *The European Right: A Historical Profile*, Berkeley, 1965

Schenk, H.G., *The Aftermath of the Napoleonic Wars*, London, 1947

Smith, David, *Left and Right in Twentieth Century Europe*, New York, 1969

*Stearns, Peter, *European Society in Upheaval: Social History since 1800*, New York, 1967

— *1848: The Revolutionary Tide in Europe*, New York, 1974

Viereck, Peter, *Conservatism Revisited*, New York, 1962

Weiss, John, *The Fascist Tradition: Radical Right Wing Extremism in Modern Europe*, New York, 1967

— *Nazis and Fascists in Europe*, New York, 1969

Woodward, E.L., *Three Studies in European Conservatism*, London, 1929

*Woolf, S.J. (ed), *European Fascism*, London and New York, 1968

AUSTRIA

Blum, Jerome, *Noble Landowners and Agriculture in Austria, 1815–1848*, Baltimore, 1948

Gulick, Charles A., *Austria from Hapsburg to Hitler*, 2 vols, Berkeley, 1948

Hofmann, Josef, *Der Pfrimer-Putsch*, Graz, 1965

Jászi, Oscar, *The Dissolution of the Habsburg Monarchy*, Chicago, 1929

Jedlicka, Ludwig F. (ed), *Die Erhebung der österreichischen Nationalsozialisten im Juli, 1934*, Vienna, 1965

*Kissinger, Henry, *A World Restored*, New York, 1964

Macartney, C.A., *The Habsburg Empire, 1790–1918*, London, 1968

MacDonald, Mary, *The Republic of Austria, 1918–1934*, London, 1946

May, Arthur J., *The Habsburg Monarchy, 1867–1914*, Cambridge, Mass., 1960

Redlich, Josef, *Emperor Francis Joseph of Austria*, London, 1929

Reimann, Viktor, *Zu gross für Österreich: Seipel und Bauer im Kampf um die Erste Republik*, Vienna, 1968

*Schorske, Carl E., 'Politics in a New Key: An Austrian Triptych', *Journal of Modern History* xxxix, No 4, 1967, pp. 342–86

Srbik, Heinrich von, *Metternich*, 3 vols, Munich, 1925–35

Strong, David F., *Austria: Transition from Empire to Republic*, New York, 1939

*Taylor, A.J.P., *The Habsburg Monarchy, 1809–1918*, London, 1948

*Whiteside, Andrew G., *Austrian National Socialism Before 1918*, The Hague, 1962

FRANCE

Aron, Robert, *The Vichy Régime*, London and New York, 1958

Artz, Frederick B., *France Under the Bourbon Restoration*, New York, 1931

Bagge, Dominique, *Les Idées politiques en France sous la Restauration*, Paris, 1952

Baldensperger, F., *Le Mouvement des idées dans l'émigration française, 1789–1815*, 2 vols, Paris, 1925

Barbé, M., *Etude historique des idées sur la souveraineté en France de 1815 à 1848*, Paris, 1904

Bardèche, Maurice, *Qu'est-ce que la fascisme?*, Paris, 1961

*Beach, Vincent Woodrow, *Charles X of France*, Boulder, Colo., 1971

Beauvoir, Simone de, 'La Pensée de droite, aujourd'hui', *Les Temps Modernes* x, 1955, pp. 1539–75, 2220–63

Beik, Paul H., 'The Revolution Seen From the Right, 1789–99', *Transactions of the American Philosophical Society* 46, Philadelphia, 1956

*Binion, Rudolph, *Defeated Leaders: The Political Fate of Caillaux, Jouvenel, and Tardieu*, New York, 1960

Blanchard, M., *The Second Empire*, Paris, 1950

Buthmann, W.C., *The Rise of Integral Nationalism in France*, New York, 1939

Byrnes, Robert F., *Antisemitism in Modern France*, New Brunswick, 1950

Chapman, Guy, *The Dreyfus Case*, London, 1965

Charléty, S., *La Restauration, 1815–1830*, Paris, 1921

Chavardès, Maurice, *Le 6 février 1934*, Paris, 1966

Chesnelong, C., *La Campagne monarchique d'octobre 1873*, Paris, 1895

Crowe, E. E., *History of the Reigns of Louis XVIII and Charles X*, 2 vols, London, 1854

Curtis, M., *Three Against the Third Republic*, Princeton, 1959

*Dansette, Adrienne, *Le Boulangisme, 1886–90*, Paris, 1938

*Darbon, Michel, *Le Conflit entre la droite et la gauche dans le catholicisme français, 1830–1953*, Toulouse, 1953

Dominique, P., *Marianne et les prétendents*, Paris, 1934

Duroselle, Jean B., *Les Débuts du catholicisme social en France, 1822–70*, Paris, 1951

Elbow, Matthew H., *French Corporative Theory, 1798–1948*, New York, 1953

*Girardet, Raoul, *La Société militaire dans la France contemporaine, 1815–1939*, Paris, 1953

Godechot, Jacques, *La Contre-révolution. Doctrine et action, 1789–1804*, Paris, 1961

*Goguel, François, *La Politique des partis sous la IIIe République*, 2 vols, Paris, 1958

Halasz, Nicholas, *Captain Dreyfus*, New York, 1955

*Halévy, Daniel, *La Fin des notables*, Paris, 1930

Herzog, Wilhelm, *From Dreyfus to Pétain*, New York, 1947

Hudson, Nora, *Ultra-Royalism and the French Revolution*, Cambridge, Mass., 1936

Johnson, Douglas, *France and the Dreyfus Affair*, London and New York, 1966

Labasse, Jean, *Hommes de droit, Hommes de gauche*, Paris, 1947

Loth, Arthur, *L'Echec de la restauration monarchique en 1873*, Paris, 1910

Lucas-Dubreton, M., *The Restoration and the July Monarchy*, London and New York, 1929

Massis, Henri, *Maurras et notre temps*, 2 vols, Paris, 1951

Mellon, Stanley, *The Political Uses of History: A Study of Historians in the French Revolution*, Stanford, 1958

Micaud, Charles, *The French Right and Nazi Germany, 1933–39*, Durham, N.C., 1943

Miéville, H.L., *La Pensée de Maurice Barrès*, Paris, 1934

Miquel, Pierre, *Poincaré*, Paris, 1961

Moulinié, Henri, *De Bonald*, Paris, 1915

Muret, Charlotte T., *French Royalist Doctrines Since the Revolution*, New York, 1933

Néré, J., *Le Boulangisme et la presse*, Paris, 1964

Oechslin, J.J., *Le Mouvement ultra-royaliste sous la Restauration*, Paris, 1960

Osgood, Samuel, *French Royalism under the Third and Fourth Republics*, The Hague, 1960

*Palmer, R.R., *Catholics and Unbelievers in Eighteenth Century France*, Princeton, 1939

Paxton, Robert O., *Parades and Politics at Vichy: The French Officer Corps under Marshal Pétain*, Princeton, 1968

*— Vichy France, New York, 1972

Phillips, Charles S., The Church in France, 1798–1849, London, 1929

Piou, J., Le Comte Albert de Mun, Paris, 1925

Plumyène, J., Pétain, Paris, 1972

*Plumyène, J., and R. Lasierra, Le Complexe de droite, Paris, 1969

— Les Fascismes français, 1923–1963, Paris, 1963

*Remond, René, The Right Wing in France: From 1815 to de Gaulle, Philadelphia, 1968

Resnick, Daniel P., The White Terror and the Political Reaction After Waterloo, Cambridge, Mass., 1966

Richard, M., Le Bonapartism sous la République, Paris, 1883

Rollet, Henri, Albert de Mun et le parti catholique, Paris, 1947

Rothkrug, Lionel, Opposition to Louis XIV, Princeton, 1965

Rudeaux, Philippe, Les Croix de Feu et le P.S.F., Paris, 1967

*Sauvigny, Bertier de, The Bourbon Restoration, Philadelphia, 1966

Shapiro, David (ed), The Right in France, 1890–1919, London, 1962

Simpson, Frederick A., Louis Napoleon and the Recovery of France, 1848–56, London and New York, 1951

Sorlin, Pierre, 'La Croix' et les Juifs, 1880–1899, Paris, 1967

*Soucy, Robert, Fascism in France: The Case of Maurice Barrès, Berkeley and London, 1972

— 'France, Veterans' Politics Between the Wars', in Stephan R. Ward (ed), The War Generation, New York, 1975

— 'The Nature of Fascism in France', Journal of Contemporary History I, 1966

Stewart, John Hall, The Restoration Era in France, 1814–1830, Princeton, 1968

*Tannenbaum, Edward R., The Action Française, London and New York, 1962

*Tilly, Charles, The Vendée, Cambridge, Mass., 1964

Tudesq, A.J., Les Grands notables en France, 1840–49, 2 vols, Bordeaux, 1964

Vidalenc, Jean, Les Emigrés français, Caen, 1963

*Weber, Eugen, Action Française: Royalism and Reaction in Twentieth Century France, Stanford, 1962

— The Nationalist Revival In France, 1905–1914, Berkeley, 1959

*Wright, Gordon, Rural Revolution in France, Stanford, 1964

GERMANY

*Allen, William Sheridan, The Nazi Seizure of Power, Chicago, 1965

Anderson, Eugene N., The Social and Political Conflict in Prussia, 1858–1864, New York, 1968

Aris, R., History of Political Thought in Germany from 1789 to 1815, London, 1936

Benz, Richard, Die deutsche Romantik, Leipzig, 1937

Bieber, H., Der Kampf um die Tradition, 1830–1880, Stuttgart, 1928

*Bracher, Karl Dietrich, Die Auflösung der weimarer Republik, Villingen, 1960

— Die deutsche Diktatur: Entstehung, Struktur, Folgen des Nationalsozialismus, Cologne/Berlin, 1969

Bramsted, Ernest K., Aristocracy and the Middle Classes in Germany, Chicago, 1964

Brinkman, C., 'Die Aristokratie im Kapitalischen Zeitalter', Grundriss der Sozialökonomik IX, 1926, Tübingen

*Bullock, Alan, Hitler: A Study in Tyranny, London and New York, 1964

Craig, Gordon, The Politics of the Prussian Army, New York, 1955

Demeter, K., Das Deutsche Offiziercorps in seinen historisch-soziologischen Grundlagen, Berlin, 1930

Droz, Jacques, Le Romanticisme politique en Allemagne, Paris, 1963

Eichendorff, J.V., 'Der Adel und die Revolution', Sämtliche Werke, Regensburg, 1911

*Endres, F.C., 'Soziologische Struktur und dazu gehörige Ideologien vor dem Weltkriege', Archiv für Sozialwissenschaft und Sozialpolitik 53, Tübingen, 1924

*Epstein, Klaus, The Genesis of German Conservatism, Princeton, 1966

Esenwein-Rothe, Ingeborg, Die Wirtschaftsverbände von 1933 bis 1945, Berlin, 1965

Eyck, Erick, Bismarck and the German Empire, London, 1958

*Fischer, Fritz, Krieg der Illusionen: Die deutsche Politik von 1911 bis 1914, Düsseldorf, 1969

Frank, Walter, Hofprediger Adolf Stoecker und die christlichsoziale Bewegung, Hamburg, 1935

*Gillis, John, The Prussian Bureaucracy in Crisis, 1840–1860, Stanford, 1971

Gollwitzer, H., Die Standesherren, Stuttgart, 1957

Grunberger, Richard, The Twelve Year Reich, New York, 1967

Guérin, Daniel, Fascism and Big Business, New York, 1939

Hallgarten, W., Vorkriegsimperialismus, Paris, 1935

*Hamerow, Theodore S., *Restoration, Revolution, and Reaction, 1815–1871*, Princeton, 1958

Herr, Friedrich, 'Der Konservative und die Reaktion', *Die Neue Rundschau* 69, No 1, 1958, pp. 490–527

Hertzman, Lewis, *DNVP: Right Wing Opposition in the Weimar Republic*, Lincoln, Nebr., 1963

Jordan, E., *Die Entstehung der konservativen Partei und die preussischen Agrarverhältnisse von 1848*, Munich, 1914

*Kehr, Eckart, *Der Primat der Innenpolitik*, Berlin, 1965
— *Schlachtflottenbau und Parteipolitik, 1894–1901*, Berlin, 1930

Klemperer, Klemens von, *Germany's New Conservatism*, Princeton, 1957

Kogon, Eugen, *The Theory and Practice of Hell*, London and New York, 1950

Kuehnl, Reinhard, *Die Nationalsozialistische Linke, 1925–30*, Meisenheim, 1966

Lewy, Guenter, *The Catholic Church and Nazi Germany*, London and New York, 1964

Liebe, Werner, *Die Deutschnationale Volkspartei, 1918–24*, Düsseldorf, 1956

Lotze, A., *Geschichte des Deutschen Beamtentums*, Berlin, 1909

*Mason, T. W., 'Some Origins of the Second World War', *Past and Present*, No 29, December 1964, pp. 67–89

*Mosse, George L., *The Crisis of German Ideology*, New York, 1964

Neumann, S., *Die Stufen des preussischen Konservatismus*, Berlin, 1930

Ompteda, G., *Deutscher Adel um 1900*, 3 vols, Berlin, 1901–2

Petersdorf, H. von, *König Friedrich Wilhelm IV*, Stuttgart, 1900.

Ponsenby, A., *The Decline of Aristocracy*, London, 1912

*Puhle, Hans-Juergen, *Agrarische Interessenpolitik und preussicher Konservatismus im wilhelmischen Reich, 1893–1914*, Hanover, 1967

Roehl, J.C.G., *Germany Without Bismarck*, London, 1967

*Schoenbaum, David, *Hitler's Social Revolution*, New York, 1966

Schueddekopf, O. E., *Linke Leute von rechts*, Stuttgart, 1960

*Schweitzer, Arthur, *Big Business in the Third Reich*, Indiana, 1964

Simon, Walter, *The Failure of the Prussian Reform Movement, 1807–1819*, Ithaca, N.Y., 1955

Southeimer, Kurt, *Antidemokratische Denken in der weimarer Republik*, Munich, 1962

*Stern, Fritz, *The Politics of Cultural Despair*, Berkeley, 1961

Taylor, A.J.P., *Bismarck: The Man and the Statesman*, London and New York, 1955

Toennies, F., 'Deutscher Adel im 19 Jahrhundert', *Neue Rundschau* II, Berlin, 1912

Waite, Robert G.L., *Vanguard of Nazism: The Free Corps Movement in Postwar Germany, 1918–23*, Cambridge, Mass., 1952

Wertheimer, Mildred, *The Pan-German League, 1890–1914*, New York, 1924

Wheeler-Bennett, John W., *The Nemesis of Power: The German Army in Politics, 1918–1945*, London, 1953

Whiteside, Andrew G., 'The Nature and Origins of National Socialism', *Journal of Central European Affairs* XVII, No. 1, April 1957, pp. 48–73

Zechlin, Egmont, *Staatsstreichpläne Bismarcks und Wilhelm II, 1890–1914*, Stuttgart/Berlin, 1929

PHOTOGRAPHIC ACKNOWLEDGMENTS

Badischer Kunstverein, Karlsruhe, 46; Bibliothèque Nationale, Paris, 6; British Library, London, 3, 7, 15–16, 21–23, 31, 33–34, 41–42; British Museum, London, 5, 12, 14, 17–20, 26–30; Deutsche Fotothek, Dresden, 37; Hermitage, Leningrad, 8; Kunsthalle, Hamburg, 9; Landesmuseum, Trier, 4; Library of Congress, Washington, 43–44; Dr Sigrid Metken, Paris, 11; Musée des Arts et Traditions Populaires, Paris, 2; Museen für Kunst und Kulturgeschichte, Lübeck, 10; Osterreichische Nationalbibliothek, Vienna, 13, 35–36; Roger-Viollet, Paris, 25, 32, 39–40; Staatliche Galerie, Dessau, 1; Victoria and Albert Museum, London, 24, 38; Zentralinstitut für Kunstgeschichte, Munich, 45, 47–48; Yugoslav Information Service, 50.

INDEX